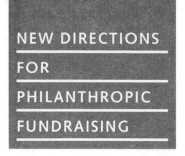

Robert E. Fogal
*Ohio Presbyterian Retirement Services Foundation*
Dwight F. Burlingame
*Indiana University Center on Philanthropy*
EDITORS

# ETHICS IN FUNDRAISING

## PUTTING VALUES INTO PRACTICE

Marianne G. Briscoe
*Hayes Briscoe Associates*

EDITOR

NUMBER 6, WINTER 1994

ETHICS IN FUNDRAISING: PUTTING VALUES INTO PRACTICE
*Marianne G. Briscoe* (ed.)
New Directions for Philanthropic Fundraising, No. 6, Winter 1994
*Robert E. Fogal, Dwight F. Burlingame*, Editors

Microfilm copies of issues and articles are available in 16 mm and 35 mm, as well as microfiche in 105 mm, through University Microfilms Inc., 300 North Zeeb Road, Ann Arbor, Michigan 48106-1346.

ISSN 1072-172X    ISBN 0-7879-9995-4

NEW DIRECTIONS FOR PHILANTHROPIC FUNDRAISING is part of The Jossey-Bass Nonprofit Sector Series and is published quarterly by Jossey-Bass Inc., Publishers, 350 Sansome Street, San Francisco, California 94104-1342.

SUBSCRIPTIONS: Please see Ordering Information at back of book.

EDITORIAL CORRESPONDENCE should be sent to Robert E. Fogal, Ohio Presbyterian Retirement Services Foundation, OMNI Plaza, 4502 Darrow Rd., Rte. 91, Stow, OH 44224-1887.

 Manufactured in the United States of America on Lyons Falls Pathfinder Tradebook. This paper is acid-free and 100 percent totally chlorine-free.

# Contents

Aristotle, Immanuel Kant, Jeremy Bentham, and John Stuart Mill each thought about ethics in ways that suggest a major role for fundraisers in the moral development of individuals.

A fundraiser's job is to participate in the creation of the gift economy in all its complexity, not just to facilitate the movement of checks or the transformation of checks into services.

The fundraising profession must be more than a collection of techniques built on a body of knowledge; it is a moral commitment, a vocation to serve public ends and values.

How can a fundraiser set forth and practice a personal set of professional ethics? What elements should those standards include?

Nonprofit organizations must build their own ethical codes. It is the board's responsibility to do this. Here are some guidelines.

Professions that serve and support nonprofit management and fundraising have their own ethical dilemmas. Fundraisers need to understand them and recognize areas, like compensation methods, where practices and principles can conflict.

# Editor's Notes

MY FRIENDS took wicked pleasure in challenging me about this work as it was in progress. They wondered if "ethics and fundraising" were not an oxymoron and how I could edit a book on such a topic. I laughed with them, but I also thought how badly this and similar books must be needed if, like the law, my profession has become such a public joke.

The examination of the fundraising profession in the moral life of a civil society is thus the topic of the first three chapters in this volume. Michael O'Neill, Marilyn Fischer, and Paul Pribbenow help us move beyond should/should not thinking about ethical fundraising to the core social values that justify and undergird the work of fundraising. These chapters are meant to give fundraisers a better and more elevated view of their work as much as to help their donors, bosses, and friends understand that fundraising may be difficult work, but it is certainly not "dirty" work.

The remaining five chapters deal with ethics and the practical issues of fundraising. Barbara Marion offers a framework for fundraisers to use in ethical decision making. Jane Geever describes how organizations, with the leadership of their boards, can establish their institutional codes of ethics. Janis Zivic considers the ethics of a related profession, executive search, and how its ethics confirm and conflict with the values of nonprofit managers and fundraisers. Beverly Goodwin explores one of the most debated areas of fundraising ethics: donor research. I then discuss some of the challenges and responsibilities managers must face to provide their staff, donors, bosses, and volunteers a sound, ethical environment for fundraising.

It is the fate, and I hope the achievement, of this volume to leave the reader hungry for more. O'Neill, Fischer, and Pribbenow can hardly do more than pose provocative questions about the aspirational values of the fundraising profession. Much thinking and

NEW DIRECTIONS FOR PHILANTHROPIC FUNDRAISING, NO. 6, WINTER 1994 © JOSSEY-BASS PUBLISHERS

discussion remains to be done about how we can assume this larger role with greater effectiveness. And we will surely encounter those who see such thinking as self-serving self-aggrandizement. How will we justify this new view of ourselves?

When it comes to ethical decision making, the contributors agree that the rules and codes are only the starting point and that the real work of ethics begins in situations where right is not clear from wrong. In preparing this volume there was one discussion among the authors in which we remembered the "situation ethics" fad of earlier decades—a viewpoint that argued that right and wrong were largely relative. The situation determined the right course of action. Were we advocating the same "cop out"? This group concluded that the power and complexity of ethics study is that ethics is a practice of the mind. Ethics do vary according to the particular situation, and relativism is an inevitable part of ethical analysis. In short, it is fine to begin an ethics discussion with "It depends." But discussion cannot end there.

In the chapters on nonprofit management and fundraising practice we faced a surfeit of possible subjects. There are essays yet to be written on planned giving, gift accounting, conflict of interest, "tainted" money, and dozens of other subjects. Further, in writing on the topics we did select for this volume, we did not intend to offer directives; our goal has been to allow readers to think more incisively about the issues. The volume as a whole has similar limitations. It can open only a few subjects in the vast domain of ethics and philanthropy, and, like the subject of ethics itself, it sets out many questions and few straightforward answers. We will be pleased if readers challenge our views—or wish there had been more. Raising the level and frequency of discussion about ethics and fundraising has been our primary goal.

Marianne G. Briscoe
*Editor*

MARIANNE G. BRISCOE *is founding principal in Hayes Briscoe Associates, a consulting firm specializing in nonprofit governance, planning, and fund development. She is also an adjunct faculty member at the University of San Francisco's Institute for Nonprofit Organization Management and a contributing editor for ethics at* NonProfit Times.

*Discussions of ethics often take a narrow and negative approach. The young profession of fundraising should heed the ancient and rich tradition of philosophical and religious ethics.*

# 1

# Fundraising as an ethical act

## Michael O'Neill

MOST DISCUSSION of ethics is narrow and negative, as if morality were worth talking about only when people are immoral. In the media and at the marketplace, people talk about ethics when a corporation hides information on the harmful effects of its products, when a government official gets caught with his or her hand in the till, when Father X or Reverend Y or Rabbi Z fools around with a member of the congregation.

If discussion of ethics in general is narrow and negative, discussion of ethics in fundraising is doubly so. The usual topics are lying about the cause, accepting tainted money, using high-pressure tactics, misusing prospect information, concealing fundraising costs, raising money on commission, and so forth. These are real problems—where there is money, there will always be temptation and often sin—but the ethics of fundraising deserves broader, deeper, and less sin-oriented reflection. One way to do this is to examine the relevance of general ethical theory to fundraising. There is no reason why the young profession of fundraising should ignore the

Adapted from *Advancing Philanthropy*, National Society of Fund Raising Executives, Alexandria, Virginia, copyright 1994. Used by permission.

NEW DIRECTIONS FOR PHILANTHROPIC FUNDRAISING, NO. 6, WINTER 1994 © JOSSEY-BASS PUBLISHERS

ancient and rich tradition of philosophical and religious ethics. The potential relevance of that tradition may be illustrated by a brief foray into three great ethical theories—Aristotle's, Immanuel Kant's, and the utilitarian theory of Jeremy Bentham and John Stuart Mill—as well as some major themes found in all ethical systems.

## Fundraisers can serve as moral trainers

Aristotle said that we are born with the *capacity* for virtue but not with virtue itself; that can be developed only through repeated virtuous acts (*Nichomachean Ethics*, Book II, Ch. 1; 1103a14–1103b25). By telling the truth we become truthful; by repeatedly showing courage we become courageous. He also taught that virtue stands in the middle, atop the difficult peak of human behavior; in the chasms on either side lie vices (*Nichomachean Ethics*, Book II, Ch. 1; 1119b21–1122a19). He uses the virtue of generosity as an example: a person who gives well and wisely is generous; a person who gives nothing or too little is miserly; a person who gives too much is irresponsible. Generosity, we might add, is important in any society and extremely important in a society such as the United States, where human needs far outstrip the capabilities of families and the will of government. Aristotle noted that generosity is not something that comes easily or automatically to most people: "most men are fonder of getting money than of giving" (*Nichomachean Ethics*, Book IV, Ch. 1; 1120a17–1120a19). Most of us have to be pushed, prodded, motivated, led. Moral virtue, he held, is developed by training. We can add that in the case of generosity, there are various trainers—parents, one would hope; religious leaders; friends; spouses; and so forth. But the need for generosity in society is so great, the potential so great, and the trainers so few—and are being weakened all the time—that more help is needed. The relatively new profession of fundraising has, in this sense, added to the societal pool of moral trainers. Fundraisers give people needed opportunities and incentives to practice generous acts and therefore become generous.

They also help people make good decisions about giving. As Aristotle noted, the virtue of generosity means not just giving, but giving to the right persons in the right amounts at the right time, and even with pleasure. (Aristotle continually insists, somewhat counterintuitively, that virtue is accompanied by pleasure, not pain.) At their best, fundraisers help people give wisely and well, avoiding the pitfalls or vices of miserliness on the one hand and irresponsibility on the other. The former is more familiar, but most fundraisers have also dealt with the latter, deterring people from giving away too much of their limited resources.

## Fundamental relationship between fundraising and moral development

Aristotle taught that the ultimate goal of ethics was happiness, and that happiness came primarily from the full exercise of one's faculties along lines of excellence, a phrase that John F. Kennedy loved to quote (*Nichomachean Ethics*, Book I, Ch. 6; 1096a11–1097a14; Book X, Ch. 6–9, 1176a30–1181b24). Happiness, Aristotle said, assumes a reasonable amount of material and social goods—a home, a certain amount of money, family, friends; but most of all happiness depends on the development and exercise of the moral and intellectual virtues, for they pertain most closely to the nature of human beings. It is somewhat pleasurable to wiggle your big toe, but it is more pleasurable to run, and more pleasurable still to talk with friends, listen to music, read, think, help someone in need. The closer you get to the essence of being human, the more potential for happiness there is.

Fundraisers often help people with means raise their sights a little, become better human beings, focus less on material and social goods and more on intellectual and moral virtue—in other words, exercise their faculties along lines of excellence. Throughout history many people have amassed great wealth, but few have seriously attempted to use their wealth to benefit society, as did Andrew

Carnegie, Margaret Olivia Sage, the Rockefeller family, and the Haas family of the Levi Strauss fortune. These individuals, unlike most rich people, rose above the simple accumulation of wealth and sought to use wealth in what Aristotle would call a virtuous manner, to make full use of their faculties along lines of excellence. These people shared their wealth largely on their own initiative, but most rich people could use a little push. Enter the fundraiser.

This is not to say that fundraisers are therefore virtuous people; they may or may not be. The point is that the *act*, or practice, of fundraising has moral significance: some dimensions of the fundraising act are fundamentally and directly related to moral or ethical development, whatever actually happens in individual cases.

---

## Charitable giving and the maxim of altruism

Immanuel Kant expressed his famous "categorical imperative" in this way: "Act in such a way that you would want the maxim, the underlying principle, of your action to become a universal law" (*Foundations*, 402, 403, 421, 423–424, 432, 436–437). Thus, you repay money you have borrowed because you would want everyone to act the same (especially everyone who owed you money). The maxim underlying your action is that everyone who owes money should repay it. Kant notes that the best way to test a maxim is to imagine the effect of its opposite. The ethical power of the maxim, "One should always tell the truth," is revealed by reflection on the consequences of everyone lying at will: trust in personal relations would end; society would be in chaos. A maxim is unethical if, led to its logical conclusion, it self-destructs.

Similarly, the ethical power of the altruism maxim, "One should help others, share one's goods with others," may be tested by imagining the effect of its opposite, "One should keep all of one's own goods at all costs." A world without charity, without altruism, would, humanly speaking, self-destruct. The maxim of altruism is not an easy one and is far from being a universal practice, but the spread of that maxim, the effort to make it more universally accepted, is certainly a work of ethics.

The cultivation of the general habit of altruism—not only the solicitation of this particular gift at this time—is, of course, an important part of the work of fundraisers. The very word "cultivation" implies this: one must get used to the idea of giving and then become more and more accustomed to giving through progressively more generous gifts, before the maxim underlying a charitable act is fully realized, before it truly becomes willed as a universal law.

Kant's second great ethical principle is "Act so that you treat humanity, whether in your own person or in that of another, always as an end and never as a means only" (*Foundations*, 429). He elaborates, "Everything has either a price or a dignity" (*Foundations*, 434), that is, either relative worth or absolute worth. The idea that only human beings have absolute worth, that material goods have only relative worth, has clear implications for the fundraiser's role.

## *Fundraisers can bring great good to great numbers of people*

The utilitarians Bentham and Mill were uncomfortable with Aristotle's assumption of a definable human nature and thought that Kant was too idealistic. Bentham and Mill wanted a more concrete and measurable basis of ethics, so they taught that ethics equals the greatest good for the greatest number of people. If your action will bring more pleasure than pain to more people, it is good; otherwise, it is bad. Far from being selfish hedonism, this theory, according to its proponents, called human beings to put the good of the community before their own personal good: What will bring the greatest good to the greatest number, and therefore how should I act?

The ethical theory of utilitarianism relates directly to the fundraiser's task. The ethical imperative here is acting to produce the greatest good for the greatest number of human beings. It would be harder to imagine an ethical rule more supportive of the fundraiser's work. Bentham (1789) defines "utility" as "that property in any object, whereby it tends to produce benefit, advantage, pleasure, good, or happiness or to prevent the happening of mischief, pain, evil, or unhappiness" (*Introduction*, Chapter I, 4). What is ethical is that which produces the greater utility for the community, what will bring about more good and alleviate more harm for more people, including oneself, of course. Most fundraisers try to obtain money to support projects that bring pleasure and alleviate pain for great numbers of people. The pleasures sought may be physical healing, educational growth, artistic enjoyment, environmental safety; the pains fought may be discrimination, homelessness, mental illness, poverty.

### Fundraisers can redistribute power

General themes found in every ethical theory also throw light on the ethics of fundraising. The ethical significance of power is one example. Many persons are in relationships that, by definition, are based on an imbalance of power: parents, teachers, doctors, psychiatrists, lawyers, and employers. Asymmetry of power has important ethical consequences. For instance, flirtation—making sexual advances—is common to both sexes and all ages; it is common to both human and animal kingdoms; it is a behavior probably millions of years old; and it even seems necessary for the biological preservation of the species. One could hardly find something more clearly written into the human genetic code than flirtation. But flirting with a new acquaintance at a party is one thing, and making sexual advances toward one's secretary, counseling client, student, or child is quite another. Another example is job separation. Ethically, and in most states legally, society puts far more burden on the employer than on the employee when it comes to the separation between a job-holder and an organization. A job-holder can occasionally hurt an organization by quitting, but typically the job-holder needs the organization—the job, the salary, the sense of self-worth—much more than the organization needs the job-holder. That is, the employer is in a position of power and thus must take greater pains to be fair toward the employee.

Fundraising is significantly related to power in society. Wealthy and powerful individuals and institutions—Exxon, the federal government, Bill Gates, David Packard—don't fundraise; they have plenty of money and ways of getting more. While there are important exceptions, most fundraising is for society's weaker, less affluent members—Salvation Army, United Way, international relief organizations, beneficiaries of religious philanthropy, and the like. So part of what fundraisers do, cumulatively, is help redistribute power in the society. Certainly that's not always the effect of fundraising, and fundraising has far less redistributive potential than the government's taxation system, but at $125 billion a year in charitable gifts, as the man said, "It's not nothin'."

The Ford Foundation is a striking if complex example of the redistributive potential of philanthropy and fundraising. In the 1930s the Ford family was one of the richest, most powerful families in the United States. Anyone who has studied the political opinions of Henry Ford understands that this very rich, powerful family was not always a positive force in American society. Facing the threat of new inheritance taxes, which Congress passed with families like Ford's very much in mind, Henry Ford created the Ford Foundation in 1936—not as a liberal, generous, high-minded act, but as a mechanism to keep control of the Ford Motor Company within the family. But a funny thing happened on the way to the forum. After Henry and Edsel Ford died, and after all the governmental and legal dust had settled, Henry Ford II decided to make the Foundation a mechanism of social betterment. So in 1951, when the Ford Foundation *really* began, with an endowment that, overnight, made it bigger than the Rockefeller Foundation and the Carnegie Corporation combined, Ford embarked on a process of grantmaking that had the effect of significant redistribution of power: the creation of hundreds of minority rights organizations, of public radio and television, of public interest law firms, of community development experiments that led to many of the Great Society programs, the support for the

"Green Revolution," the support that helped turn around the economy of India, and so forth. The Ford Foundation could have remained a highly selfish, small-minded, family-centered operation (several examples come to mind) or, perhaps as futile, could have disappeared into the revenue machine of the federal government. Its turn to altruism, and the redistribution of power that this set in motion, constitute a example of the ethical significance of such acts.

There's another sense in which fundraising has to do with power. Many of the causes for which people raise money—education, physical and mental health care, equal opportunity for minorities and women, and so forth—have to do with empowering people: "micro-power," as distinguished from the macro-power of the Ford Foundation example. Micro-power is very important, in two senses. First, for the individuals directly affected: as someone has said, chicken feed is greatly appreciated by the chickens. The empowerment of just one human being is a deeply important thing. Second, cumulative micro-power becomes macro-power: all those individuals educated, trained, healed, freed, encouraged. Fundraising, indirectly as always, has much to do with the delicate balance of power in human relationships, that constant source of ethical challenge.

Certainly not all but many instances of philanthropy lead to a healthy redistribution of power in society; and to the extent that fundraisers make that happen, they are engaged, it seems to me, in profoundly ethical work.

---

## Fundraisers can enable humans to feel responsible for one another

Another factor that introduces ethics into the human situation is responsibility. This clearly applies to most if not all asymmetrical power relationships such as parent-child, teacher-student, counselor-client, but it also applies to relationships between equals, such as spouse to spouse, sister to sister, soldier to soldier, friend to friend, parishioner to parishioner, worker to coworker, and so forth.

The Latin poet very beautifully said to his lover, "You have become the *dimidium animae meae*, the other half of my soul," but even in less intense relationships we become part of each other in some way—Australians say "mates," soldiers say "buddies," the women's movement has given new meaning to the word "sisterhood," and so forth. When we become part of each other, we assume a certain responsibility for each other. This is not just a legalistic thing. The Latin root of "responsibility" is *spondere*, which means "to promise solemnly, to pledge, to vow"; it is also the root of the English word "spouse." It's interesting that in spite of all the flag-waving of all nations throughout history, the almost universal report of soldiers on the battlefield is that, when the chips are down, they fight not for their country or their flag or some ideal but for each other, for other human beings that they can see and hear and touch and for whom they feel responsibility.

Responsibility begins with those closest to us, those who have become in some way "the other half of our soul," but it extends outward, in a series of concentric circles. As we grow ethically, we come to feel responsibility to our neighbors, our city, our organization, our profession, our ethnic or religious group, our country, even our world; we come to feel responsible even to abstract ideals like truth, beauty, and honor. We not only feel such things; we behave in remarkable ways out of such feelings and commitments. People give their time, their talents, their worldly goods, sometimes even their lives, out of such feelings of responsibility.

Fundraisers deal constantly with responsibility, in at least two important ways: First, they create or help create feelings of responsibility—for political prisoners, for starving children, for the mentally ill. Second, fundraisers connect already existing feelings of responsibility with opportunities for responding. In poll after poll Americans have said that they would give more if asked, that the primary reason they don't give, or don't give more, is that they're not asked. In other words, fundraisers help connect the supply of charitable feelings with the demand for charitable dollars, balancing the equation of human responsibility.

## *Fundraisers can break down our natural selfishness*

A third factor that creates ethical dimensions is more elusive than power or responsibility, but probably more important. It is the paradox of "becoming what you are" as a human person. Aristotle described this paradox when he said, "Moral excellence is the result of habit. The virtues are not implanted in us by nature, but nature gives us the capacity for acquiring them, and this is accomplished by training" (*Nichomachean Ethics*, Book II, Ch. 1; 1103a14–1103a25). St. Augustine in his *Confessions* described the same impulse in a religious context, saying to God, "Thou hast made us for Thyself, and our hearts are restless till they rest in Thee." Kant described the paradox when he said that to be moral, a human being must become a quasi-divine lawgiver: "Man is subject only to his own, yet universal, legislation, and he is bound to act in accordance with his own will, which is, however, designed by nature to be a will giving universal laws" (*Introduction*, 432). And Jean-Paul Sartre, explaining existential *angst*, wrote: "The man who involves himself and who realizes that he is not only the person he chooses to be, but also a lawmaker who is, at the same time, choosing all mankind as well as himself, cannot help escape the feeling of his total and deep responsibility" (1957, p. 31). The work of fundraising is clearly related to this phenomenon, in that at its best it assists people in responding to the deep ethical call within them, the call to go out of themselves for others.

Aristotle noted over 2,000 years ago that people prefer to get than give money, and not much has changed since. A good fundraiser helps break down that natural wall of selfishness. Fundraisers and the organizations and people they represent are an essential part of the economic and moral exchange system of American society. This should be the starting point for thinking about the ethics of fundraising, not the moral lapses and pitfalls of this work.

### *References*

Aristotle. *Nichomachean Ethics*. Berlin edition.
Augustine. *Confessions*.

Bentham, J. *An Introduction to the Principles of Morals and Legislation.* (Originally published 1789.)

Kant, I. *Foundations of the Metaphysics of Morals.* Akademie edition.

Sartre, J. P. *Existentialism and Human Emotions.* (B. Frechtman, trans.) New York: Philosophical Library, 1957.

MICHAEL O'NEILL *is professor and director of the Institute for Nonprofit Organization Management, University of San Francisco.*

*The ethics of fundraising derive in a most basic sense from the purposes and ideals of philanthropy. We can think of philanthropy as a "gift economy" in which fundraisers facilitate the movement of gifts among donors and recipients. Through sharing our gifts we create community among all participants.*

# 2

# The philanthropic community as a gift economy

*Marilyn Fischer*

FUNDRAISING ETHICS encompasses an amalgam of topics, arising from fundraisers' many, diverse responsibilities. As solicitors, fundraisers must be sensitive to issues of truth-telling, confidentiality, and privacy. They must be attuned to the needs and capabilities of colleagues, board members, volunteers, and the community. As members of institutions they must deal with the ethics of financial accountability and professionalism. As educators they need to present a vision of the public good, articulating how their organizations contribute toward realizing that vision.

Rather than trying to develop a unified theory of fundraising ethics based on the specific responsibilities of practitioners, I think it would be more fruitful to go up one level of generality to examine the purposes of philanthropy. In the first part of this chapter, I will discuss how ethical values are central to the very definition of philanthropy, and in the second part, propose "the gift economy"

NEW DIRECTIONS FOR PHILANTHROPIC FUNDRAISING, NO. 6, WINTER 1994 © JOSSEY-BASS PUBLISHERS

as a metaphor for the philanthropic community. This will give us a conceptual map upon which to locate the ethics of fundraisers' particular tasks and responsibilities.

## Ethical values and the definition of philanthropy

To understand how ethics are at the center of philanthropy's definition, we can begin by making a distinction between an ethics of obligation and an ethics of aspiration. Our ethical obligations are those duties that we would be remiss not to perform. They give a moral minimum, below which a morally decent person should not fall. Ethics codes, such as the National Society of Fund Raising Executives' (NSFRE) "Code of Ethical Principles and Standards of Professional Practice" (1992) often include a list of ethical obligations expected of all members. For example, the NSFRE code states that members will comply with the law, disclose conflicts of interest, be truthful in stating their qualifications, keep constituent information confidential, and so on. It is important that these obligations be clearly articulated and that organizations have methods for ensuring that members meet them.

But ethics encompasses more than obligations. It includes not only a moral minimum, but also a vision of our ideals, aims, and aspirations. An organization's ethical code sometimes includes statements of aspiration; for example, the NSFRE code states that its members "serve the ideal of philanthropy, are committed to the preservation and enhancement of volunteerism, and hold stewardship of these concepts as the overriding principle of professional life; . . . foster cultural diversity and pluralistic values and treat all people with dignity and respect . . ." and so on. Our service to these ideals can waver; sometimes we are ill-tempered and treat colleagues, donors, or recipients with less than dignity and respect. Ideals and aspirations can never be entirely fulfilled, yet it is important to articulate them so that we can have a clear sense of purpose and direction.

In his introduction to *Critical Issues in American Philanthropy*, Jon Van Til (1990) writes, "No single comprehensive definition of philanthropy has emerged from this book, though the field requires as much clarification in its theory, conceptualization, and practice as can humanly and reasonably be expected" (p. xx). Here the ancient Greek notion of definition is helpful. The Greeks defined things in terms of their function or purpose, believing that one cannot understand what a thing *is* without understanding what it is *for*. Now philanthropy clearly has an ethical purpose. To define philanthropy is to articulate an ethic of aspiration by identifying ethical ideals toward which we should strive.

A quick review of some definitions of philanthropy makes clear that they embody an ethic of aspiration. For example, Bremner (1988) writes, "The aim of philanthropy in its broadest sense is improvement in the quality of human life. Whatever motives animate individual philanthropists, the purpose of philanthropy itself is to promote the welfare, happiness, and culture of mankind" (p. 3). O'Connell (1987) gives us a list of what philanthropy helps us to do: "To discover new frontiers of knowledge; to support and encourage excellence; to enable people to exercise their potential; to relieve human misery; to preserve and enhance democratic government and institutions; to make communities a better place to live; to nourish the spirit; to create tolerance, understanding, and peace among people; to remember the dead" (p. 8).

In many definitions of philanthropy the notion of community is at the center. This association is deeply rooted in our history. Note John Winthrop's comment (1983) as frequently cited in the philanthropic literature: "We must delight in each other, make other's conditions our own, rejoice together, mourn together, labor and suffer together, always having before our eyes our commission and community in the work, our community as members of the same body" (p. 28).

Payton (1988) understands philanthropy as embracing two values—compassion, with its Judeo-Christian roots, and community, from the Greek and Roman traditions (p. 44). Gardner (1991) reinforces how building community is central to the work of the philanthropic sector. He speaks of community this way: "We know from a lot of evidence that community not only confers identity, but a sense of belonging and allegiance, and a sense of security. But, more important, we know that communities are the ground-level generators of values" (p. 145). He goes on to explain how the non-profit sector is eminently suited to foster the healthy growth and sustenance of communities. "What I want to say is that the sector we're concerned with—the nonprofit sector—has a very special role in bringing this about. We have the capacity to move across boundaries to knit together a lot of things that need knitting together today" (p. 148).

Van Til (1990), well aware of tensions in definitions of philanthropy, proposes that we find a "third way." He suggests, "One such approach, potentially able to transcend the divisions of prevailing paradigms, is that which sees philanthropy as essentially involving an exchange of values among people" (p. 28). In philanthropy, he says, exchange can involve transferring money or volunteer service. Sometimes these exchanges are without expectation of return (altruistic); sometimes the desired return is in terms of tax benefits, or personal or social success (p. 29).

In this chapter I take Van Til's insight regarding the concept of exchange and link it with the notion of community. This will allow us to articulate an ethic of aspiration, or more modestly, a metaphor of aspiration through which we can define or conceptualize the philanthropic sector. Metaphors are potent; they give us a way of grasping ideals, and from that, gaining insight into how to proceed in everyday actions and decisions. By developing the notion of a "gift economy" as a metaphor of aspiration, I hope to contribute to clarifying the concept of philanthropy, and thereby contribute to its practice.

## Commodity exchange and gift exchange

We usually think of exchange in terms of a market economy. According to classical market theory, in a marketplace self-interested individuals bargain with other self-interested individuals to further their own individual interests. For purposes of the exchange, they have no particular interest in their trading partners, aside from providing the opportunity to obtain what they want. Market participation is voluntary in the sense that it is not coerced legally; no one is forced to trade with any particular person or for any preestablished price. The laws of supply and demand govern the participants' interactions; thus exchange through the market economy is an orderly way for self-interested parties to further their individual interests. In theory, the exchange is between parties who need not define their ideals or aspirations in terms of each other at all. Through exchange the market does not confer identity, a sense of belonging or allegiance—the qualities Gardner ascribes to community in the quotation cited above. (In this chapter, goods exchanged through the market economy will be called "commodities." Of course, the same good can function as a commodity in one setting and as a gift in another.)

However, a market exchange is not the only kind of exchange. Lewis Hyde (1983), in his fascinating and deeply insightful book *The Gift*, offers a model of another kind of exchange, one which is lively, life-giving, and community-enriching. Using mythological stories and customs of traditional societies, Hyde uncovers the character and dynamics of gift exchange. He begins by telling the story of the Native Americans who offered a pipe to the newly arrived Puritans. It was the tradition among Native Americans to pass the pipe from tribe to tribe. It might stay with one tribe for a time, but all understood that the pipe was to be passed on. When a neighboring tribe visited the Puritans some time later, the new settlers were baffled when the visitors seemed to expect the Puritans to give them the pipe as an indication of goodwill (pp. 3–4).

In this brief story Hyde sees the meaning of a gift and the character of gift exchange. The gift is a tangible symbol of feelings between people; it must be passed on, and by its circulation it creates the bonds of community.

A gift, Hyde says, is "an emanation of eros" (p. 22). Gifts establish bonds of feeling between people. Gifts come with strings attached—strings of affection, expectation, obligation, gratitude, mutuality, friendship. The point of the gift exchange is not so much the tangible thing given, as the attachments thereby created and sustained. In giving and receiving gifts, people enmesh themselves into the lives of others. Here the contrast with commodity exchange is clear. Only the commodity is transferred from one party to another; feelings, affection, and friendship are irrelevant to the exchange. By contrast, to give or to receive a gift is to entrust oneself to the other. Giving and receiving gifts creates and manifests an interdependence in fact and in feeling.

In the Native American tradition, the pipe was always to be kept in circulation. To hold it as one's own was to violate "the spirit of the gift" (pp. 18–19). Hyde comments that the Native Americans "understood a cardinal property of the gift: whatever we have been given is supposed to be given away again, not kept. Or, if it is kept, something of similar value should move on in its stead, the way a billiard ball may stop when it sends another scurrying across the felt, its momentum transferred" (p. 4). Hyde speaks of this movement in terms of consumption: " . . . a gift is consumed when it moves from one hand to another with no assurance of anything in return" (p. 9). With the movement of the gift, the exchange is always off balance (p. 15). Now with commodity exchange, equivalents are traded, and the transaction is ended. But with gift exchange, one may in some sense expect a return, but one cannot negotiate or bargain for what the return will be, when it will come, what form it will take, or even if it will come at all. In this sense one puts oneself into the hands of the other. In gift exchange there is reciprocity throughout time, but the terms of the reciprocity are not the giver's to make.

Now we can see why Hyde speaks of gifts as "lively" and as containing "vitality" (p. 25). The gifts transmit or represent bonds of vital feeling, and because the exchange must always move and is always off balance, there is the promise that the feeling-bonds will continue to be nourished. Hyde writes, " . . . a circulation of gifts nourishes those parts of our spirit that are not entirely personal, parts that derive from nature, the group, the race or the gods. Furthermore, although these wider spirits are a part of us, they are not 'ours'; they are endowments bestowed upon us. To feed them by giving away the increase they have brought us is to accept that our participation in them brings with it an obligation to preserve their vitality" (p. 38).

Through creating bonds of feeling, through their movement among us, a gift exchange is emblematic of community. Hyde writes, "When a gift passes from hand to hand in this spirit, it becomes the binder of many wills. What gathers in it is not only the sentiment of generosity but the affirmation of individual goodwill, making of those separate parts a *spiritus mundi*, a unanimous heart, a band whose wills are focused through the lens of the gift" (p. 35). Hyde likes to think of gifts moving through a community as a cir-cle, and the circle as an expanding ego, binding people together and feeding the "wider spirits" as it moves (pp. 16–17). Gifts—not only tangible items, but also gifts of one's time and one's care—are the stuff which, to again cite Gardner, confer identity, a sense of belong-ing and allegiance, and a sense of security.

As Hyde rightly sees, except in very small traditional societies, we need both commodity and gift economies (pp. 88–89). If all exchanges brought with them bonds of feeling, members of con-temporary mass society would soon fall into emotional exhaustion. Yet if we participate only in commodity exchanges, we suffer isola-tion, alienation, and a loss of connection to others and the "wider spirits" (p. 67).

## *Philanthropic sector as a gift economy*

Overall conceptual schemes matter. The images we have in our minds of what we do, although often unconscious, influence our actions and responses. Making these images explicit can help us clarify our understanding and our aspirations. Using Hyde's under-standing of a gift economy can give us an image, a metaphor of aspi-ration, for our work in the philanthropic sector.

I heard a fundraiser once talk about her job as that of facilitating the gift, to keep it moving. That is insightful and exactly right. Here we need to understand "gift" broadly—not just the check, or the volunteer hours, but as that which moves and thereby joins the community together. A fundraiser's job is to participate in the creation of the gift economy in all its complexity, not just to facilitate the movement of checks or the transformation of checks into services.

Although Hyde draws many of his examples from an anthropological study of traditional societies, I think the gift economy can still serve as a helpful metaphor of aspiration within the context of contemporary mass society. When we think of "community" we generally envision a community of place—a neighborhood or other geographic location with houses, schools, churches, and workplaces. Thus, people decry the loss of community as traditional community structures (and the gift economies distinctive to them) diminish in importance. Communities of place are important, but in mass society we can add to them communities organized around other choices and concerns: the arts community, the academic community, various health care communities, the "improve literacy" community, and so forth. Communities of choice and concern, as well as place, can all be understood through the metaphor of the gift economy, with the philanthropic sector serving the vital and integrative function of facilitating the movement of gifts.

### Donors

Thinking about donors in terms of their place in the gift economy gives us a way to consider what sorts of motivations for giving are "ethical" or "unethical." Payton (1988) writes, "The irreducible core of the (philanthropic) sector is its voluntary dimension" (p. 61). On the surface, the connection to a gift economy is obvious—unless a gift is given voluntarily, it is not a gift. But there is a tendency to conflate "voluntary giving" with "altruistic giving." For example, in his text on fundraising, Greenfield (1991) writes, "Nearly every recorded culture has considered it noble to help someone else, especially when the giver expects nothing in return. Altruism, a devotion to others or to humanity, places the notion of giving to benefit others on a lofty level" (p. 2). While I share Greenfield's appreciation of altruism's nobility, I worry about making it so lofty. When altruism is raised to such heights, it is used both to praise and to condemn. People are praised when their actions are clearly altruistic, but faulted when other motives enter, especially when they seem to enjoy, if not expect, something in return. While altruism is certainly *a* philanthropic motive, it is not the only one, and in fact, I think it is a fragile virtue, rarely existing in isolation and often unsustainable. Donors and volunteers give for many reasons. Greenfield's list includes "charity, ego, respect, religion, recognition, participation, joining with others, helping others, and many more" (p. 11). Given the complexity of the feeling web created by gift economies, one should expect that motives and expectations will also be complex.

Now, in Hyde's understanding of a gift economy, gifts, though given voluntarily, often carry with them an expectation of return. The gift I give my child for Christmas is truly a gift, even though it is fully expected, and I would be remiss not to give it. And it is right for me to expect a gift in return, a gift not of my choosing, or necessarily of monetary equivalence to the one I gave. In the gift economy, it is not "selfish" to want or expect a return. When one is a part of a community, attached by bonds of feeling, it is a reasonable return, for the return is an indication that the gift has come full circle and that one's membership in the community is acknowledged. (And the return can take many forms—recognition, status, personal satisfaction, as well as receipt of service.)

Thinking more carefully about the role of the self in a gift economy can help us understand that altruism, while a praiseworthy motive, should not be thought of as the only, or the best, or the purest one. To give altruistically is to give selflessly. But note that selflessness is a kind of detachment. It does not enmesh the self in a community; it does not create a feeling bond of reciprocity or mutuality. Selflessness and selfishness are not opposite poles on the same continuum. Participating in a gift economy is neither selfless nor selfish. It is to be a self-in-community, an enlarging of the self through felt participation with others. Thus we should not blame or think less of donors who are not purely altruistic. While we can appreciate altruism, and seek to cultivate it, we need not hold it aloft as the highest ideal, as if somehow the most morally praiseworthy donor was the most purely altruistic one.

Thinking of gifts as bringing feeling-bonds that create community can also help us identify when motives are not philanthropic, and may in fact do the community harm. When the recipients' genuine needs are overlooked, or when the gift is given primarily for self-aggrandizement or as an attempt to exert power over others, the feeling-bonds of community are not created. Thus, it is appropriate to question the motives of a person who wants to "exchange" a large donation for a seat on the board in order to pursue her own idiosyncratic vision of what the community needs. The drug dealer who donates grandly, asking that a hospital wing be named after him, contributes funds, but does not enhance Gardner's list of community identity, belonging, allegiance, and security.

The gift exchange, in contrast with commodity exchange, can help explain why many fundraisers feel uneasy about corporate giving. Payton (1988) observes, "The rationale for corporate philanthropy has always been presented in terms of 'enlightened self-interest'" (p. 187). To give out of enlightened self-interest is to try to make a donation function as both a gift and a commodity at the same time. Yet the corporation's hope for a return is quite different from my hope that my child or sister will give me a birthday gift. The feeling-bonds of community, essential to a gift being a true gift, do not have a place in a commodity exchange. We are uneasy about enlightened self-interest because, to the extent a donation functions like a gift, it cannot function like a commodity; when it is intended as a type of commodity, it is not truly a gift.

### Recipients

The notion of a gift economy gives us a way to think about recipients, and to articulate more clearly what our ultimate aspirations for the recipients should be. The spirit of the gift is that it keep moving. This implies that a recipient will keep and use the gift for a time, and at some point will be in a position to pass it (or its equivalent) on. The metaphor of the gift economy places in a new light the familiar dictum about teaching people to fish rather than giving them fish. The goal is not simply self-sufficiency, but enabling recipients to become full-fledged participants in the gift economy.

But what of those cases where recipients are not able, and may never be able to reciprocate? This may be the place where altruism, or giving with no expectation of return, is appropriate and needed. However, we can also use this question as an occasion to think about just who the participants in a community are. Although this assumption may not be stated explicitly, in a commodity exchange, the participants are self-interested, *self-sufficient* individuals. Now, we may be self-sufficient individuals for certain portions of our lives, but all of us, at various crucial points in our lives, are vulnerable, needy, and unable to reciprocate. Gardner talks about communities as giving a sense of security. Part of that sense is knowing that one will be cared for, when needed. This casts the donor-recipient relation in a new light. Rather than seeing this relation as between the haves and the have-nots, we should think of it as one factor that creates the sort of community which cares for all of us when we need it.

### Fundraisers

Sustaining a gift economy over time takes work. In our society much of our gift economy is institutionalized in philanthropic organizations; fundraisers are critical in sustaining the gift economy through those institutions. A fundraiser's diverse responsibilities—cultivating prospects, planning special events, and so on—can be understood and unified by thinking of their contributions in sustaining the gift economy. A fundraiser is an *educator* and a *facilitator*, conveying the vision of the gift economy, and inspiring and enabling people to participate in the community of giving.

In "Fundraising as an Ethical Act" in this volume, Michael O'Neill stresses both of these roles. He speaks of the educative role, referring to fundraisers as "moral trainers," as "the new midwives of the virtue of generosity." This is moral education in the sense of helping people to become more virtuous themselves and not only encouraging them to give specific gifts to specific organizations. O'Neill also describes a fundraiser's role as a facilitator of community through creating feelings of responsibility and connecting these feelings with occasions for giving.

Understanding the philanthropic sector as a gift economy can help us in a number of ways. It gives a conceptual definition of philanthropy that incorporates key philanthropic concepts: voluntarism, community-building, and compassion in nourishing the "wider-spirits." It provides a metaphor of aspiration, articulating and clarifying our ethical ideals. It also provides a paradigm for unifying the diverse tasks a fundraiser performs. Thinking of philanthropy as a gift economy gives fundraisers a comprehensive conceptual framework within which to better understand their own professional responsibilities and standards.

## References

Bremner, R. *American Philanthropy*. (2nd ed.) Chicago: University of Chicago Press, 1988.

Gardner, J. W. "Summary of Statement to IS Committee on Values and Ethics." In *Ethics and Obedience to the Unenforceable*. Washington, D.C.: Independent Sector, 1991.

Greenfield, J. M. *Fund-Raising: Evaluating and Managing the Fund Development Process*. New York: Wiley, 1991.

Hyde, L. *The Gift: Imagination of the Erotic Life of Property*. New York: Random House, 1983.

National Society of Fund Raising Executives. "Code of Ethical Principles and Standards of Professional Practice." In *NSFRE News*, 1992, *29* (6).

O'Connell, B. *Philanthropy in Action*. New York: Foundation Center, 1987.

Payton, R. *Philanthropy: Voluntary Action for the Public Good*. New York: Macmillan, 1988.

Van Til, J., and Associates. *Critical Issues in American Philanthropy: Strengthening Theory and Practice*. San Francisco: Jossey-Bass, 1990.

Winthrop, J. "A Model of Christian Charity." In B. O'Connell (ed.), *America's Voluntary Spirit*. New York: Foundation Center, 1983.

MARILYN FISCHER *is assistant professor of philosophy at the University of Dayton, Ohio. She writes on ethics and fundraising, the concept of philanthropy, and issues involving philanthropy and justice.*

*Discussions of fundraising as a profession frequently review lists of professional traits, comparing them with the field of fundraising. This chapter focuses on the public purpose that fundraising serves, and the impact that fundraising's public role has on how fundraisers approach their work.*

# 3

# Fundraising as public service: Renewing the moral meaning of the profession

## Paul Pribbenow

THERE ARE MANY who agree with Robert Payton (1988) when he says that "There are those, on one extreme, who consider fundraising enjoyable; they are in the minority. Most people don't like to ask other people for money" (p. 63). That the public image of the fundraising profession is in such disarray is very much linked to the inescapable fact that the "currency" of our work is, in a fundamental way, *currency*.

Within the profession, our response to this public image problem often focuses on being more "professional," developing better techniques and more comprehensive codes of ethics and standards, and pursuing university-based research and training. We seem to believe that these responses somehow help to overcome the problems associated with a line of work that has to do the transfer of money, albeit for good ends. Though I find many of these efforts interesting and

NEW DIRECTIONS FOR PHILANTHROPIC FUNDRAISING, NO. 6, WINTER 1994 © JOSSEY-BASS PUBLISHERS

helpful for the profession, they ignore a more basic issue related to the reason the fundraising profession exists and the purposes it serves: promoting what I will call the public practice of philanthropy. In other words, I believe that we must reconceive the nature of our profession and its moral purposes, rather than merely tinker with its techniques. I contend that the public image problem of the fundraising profession will change only when the profession focuses its attention above all on the public goods it serves, not on the funds it raises.

In this chapter, I have two simple points to make: First, the fundraising profession (and its fellow professions in contemporary American society) needs to move away from a model that focuses primarily on private professions and embrace the public role and meaning of professional work in our society. Second, this public service model of the professions has significant implications for how the fundraising professions and individual fundraisers approach their work, both within the institutions they serve and in the wider society. I will offer a few concrete examples of these implications as a means to open dialogue that I hope can help renew the moral meaning of our work.

## Public service: Professions and the public good

Throughout this chapter, I use the term "public" primarily as the idea of a realm "in which, as free and equal citizens, we hold one another accountable for what we know in our common life" (McCollough, 1991, p. 61). I believe that professionals in America "owe" this public. That provocative claim will not meet with universal consensus in the professional community; however, it underlies my argument for the renewal of the moral meaning of professions in our society. In what follows, I will illustrate several ways of describing professionals' public obligations. Specifically, I want to draw the important distinction between serving the public interest and serving the public good—a distinction that reflects very different perspectives on how public obligations are paid.

The professions often claim that they serve the public interest. A doctor serves the public interest by treating patients. An attorney serves the public interest by representing a client. A social worker serves the public interest by helping the young single mother. The fundraiser serves the public interest by raising money for organizations that pursue important missions. Professional codes of ethics often promote service to the public interest. The public interest is not, however, the same as the public good (or common good) as is often assumed. As Frederick Reamer (1993) says, "Although these terms are used interchangeably, they have different origins and meanings" (p. 34).

The concept of public interest is based on a political philosophy that initially evolved in the seventeenth and eighteenth centuries. It became a central feature of the emerging social philosophies of liberalism, utilitarianism, and democratic pluralism. It thus also became part of the social contract theory of social relations, signifying the "aggregation of the private interests of individuals who join together in an association dedicated to the pursuit of mutual advantage" (Jennings, Callahan, and Wolf, 1987, p. 6). The principal assumption is that society is an alliance of "primarily self-interested individuals" and the public interest is promoted by "enhancing individuals' pursuit of their own interests" (Reamer, 1993, p. 35).

The concept of the public or common good, on the other hand, is based on a communal or social understanding of human nature and has its roots in ancient Greek political thought. It is "associated with a vision of society as a community whose members are joined in a shared pursuit of values and goals that they hold in common. . . ." (Jennings, Callahan, and Wolf, 1987, p. 6). It has to do with the well-being of the community and its core values, and it also pertains to the *telos* or end toward which the members of society strive together. The public good is the good of the commons, the definition of human flourishing, and the good life.

The professions and individual professionals serve the public good by bringing their distinctive and critical perspectives to bear on public discussion of basic human values and on how society defines the good life. Professionals serve the public good by being contributors and leaders in the civic discourse. Professionals and professions are "powerful shaping forces in our culture. . . .They affect not only how individuals live and how institutions work, but also the way we think about how we should live and about the ends our social institutions should serve" (Jennings, Callahan, and Wolf, 1987, p. 8).

The distinction between serving the public interest and the public good is critical to the renewal of the moral meaning of the professions. Though they might be seen as two aspects of public service, part of the same general societal dynamic, they are, in fact, very different ways of thinking about the role of professionals in society, and their differing implications may often clash. Serving the public interest means primarily serving individual needs and conceiving of one's role as individual-oriented. Serving the public good means primarily serving society and thinking about one's role as public-oriented. The public interest view signifies private interests; the public good view refers to common needs.

Another helpful way to think about this distinction between serving the public interest and the public good is offered by Elizabeth Howe (1980), who suggests that the dominant model for the professions in American society is the medical profession (p. 180 ff). She characterizes this model as "private," by which she means that professionals in this model are primarily accountable to individual clients and are granted autonomy to pursue and control their work by these clients. Whether or not this picture of the medical model is completely accurate, the case is that most professions aspire to this autonomy. Professions want to control their jurisdictions, their knowledge bases, their professional techniques, even their commitments to serve a public interest. In other words, professional work and service in our society is primarily on the professions' terms.

In juxtaposition to this private model of the professions, Howe contends that some professions are by definition and purpose primarily accountable to the public. These public professions, among which she includes social work, public administration, and urban

planning, "provide collective services and involve economic exter-
nalities that affect the public at large" (p. 179). These public professions are controlled by public needs; they are accountable to the
public for the work they do. By definition, their work and service
are on the public's terms.

I believe Howe's distinction between private and public professions is very helpful. In fact, I want to go beyond her sociological
observation that such a distinction exists to claim that there is a normative challenge in the notion of public professions that should
serve as a claim upon all professions in our society. The fundraising
profession must pursue what it would mean to take seriously the
public accountability for its work.

Robert Bellah and William Sullivan (1987) offer a helpful exten-
sion of this framework for thinking about how all professional work
is genuinely a form of public service. They remind us that the professions in modern society have come to be viewed primarily as a
market commodity, part of the capitalist economy to be sold to the
highest bidder. Professional knowledge, expertise, training, status,
and so forth all become part of the package in pursuit of greater
income and prestige. In the early twentieth century, the traditional
role of the inherited professions (medicine, law, and the clergy), and
their claims to particular moral and political expertise, became difficult to sustain. In order to deal with this difficulty, the professions
turned to an increasingly scientific and technological understanding
of professional work (p. 17). The first professional fundraisers joined
in this move as they sought to define their profession (Cutlip, 1965).

Bellah and Sullivan contend that in order to conceive of the professions in relation to public purposes, we must be able to conceive
of society in relation to the "moral bonds of trust, loyalty and
mutual concern without which contracts, laws, and even economic
exchanges threaten to turn into covert piracy and warfare" (p. 11).
In other words, in order to promote a model of professionals as servants of the public good, we must also promote an understanding
of the public that believes (and acts as if) it has a good in common.

This link between the professions and responsible citizenship is the key to understanding how we can sustain the notion that professions are forms of public service. Bellah and Sullivan define the link between the professions and responsible citizenship through the concept of "public practices," by which they mean the activities that help a society define itself, affirm its common end, and promote its life. Public practices help to sustain health, justice, welfare, education, and other public goods that undergird our common life. These practices are good in and of themselves, and are not dependent on the external goods that accrue to them. For example, the promotion of public sanitation is a public practice. It is a good thing to do, most of us would say. Though someone who promotes public sanitation might well be paid for their work and might receive some acclaim for a job well done, those external rewards do not define the practice. It is recognized as good because it serves the common good.

Professions have evolved around public practices. Social work developed as a response to the needs of the poor and troubled. The medical profession seeks to promote health. The legal profession pursues justice. Teachers serve to educate our young people. Fundraisers help support the important work of voluntary associations in our society by nurturing and sustaining philanthropy. These important objectives remain a central part of the work of these professions. The obstacles that our society puts in the way of professions pursuing these public goals have certainly deterred them, but public purposes are still present in the history and contemporary unfolding of their work in these fields. As we help professions and professionals reclaim these public practices as central to their work, we also help them become better, more effective, more responsible citizens of the national community. In their public service, the professions become "important agents in promoting citizenship as participation in the practices of common life" (Jennings, Callahan, and Wolf, 1987, p. 10).

In this chapter, the professions and individual professionals are challenged to give up their narrow claims to serve public interest and instead are urged to reclaim their historic and valuable role as servants of the public good. As professionals live out the public practices that define and give meaning to their work, they help to model an understanding of our common life that challenges the status quo and helps to create public frameworks for addressing and resolving public problems. Such work, I believe, is the proper and responsible purpose of professions in America.

---

## Promoting the public practice of philanthropy

What does this model of professions as forms of public service mean for the fundraising profession? If we agree that the primary purpose of the fundraising profession is to promote the public practice of philanthropy, then we can begin to articulate the sorts of implications this perspective might have for our day-to-day work. In the following sections, I want to suggest three abiding issues for the fundraising profession that help to illustrate this perspective.

### Fundraising knowledge and the philanthropic covenant

What do fundraisers know that others do not? The evolution of professional fundraising in the early twentieth century illustrates that the profession was a mix of other professions—advertising, public relations, and journalism, among others—and some continue to believe that fundraising is simply skills-based work rather than a profession in the real sense of the word (Bloland and Bornstein, 1991). This opinion, though correct when pertaining to the technical aspects of fundraising work, ignores the wider knowledge base and context for understanding fundraising knowledge.

What then is the *nature of professional knowledge in fundraising?* As Robert Payton tells us, "There is an abundant literature on how to raise money. It is a practical literature, written largely by practitioners. It rarely asks questions that might stir doubts or second thoughts in the minds of those it is intended to persuade" (1988, p. 63). This practical literature offers the how-to's of professional work, but seldom sets knowledge in a broader philosophical context.

I believe that a crucial strategy for developing an appropriate understanding of human society, and of professional work in that society, is to force the profession to explore the broader implications of its knowledge, to set that knowledge in conversation and dialogue with several partners, including its historical roots, its current role in the philanthropic community and wider public, and its understanding of the public good it claims to serve (Rosso, 1992).

Bloland and Bornstein (1991) argue that generating a knowledge base for the fundraising profession involves three tactics: developing a set of skills appropriate for improving fundraising capabilities, creating a theory base related to the skills, and initiating research that modifies the theory base and improves the skills (p. 114). The development of skills helps fundraisers to become more effective in their work and to gain and maintain control over work and work jurisdiction. This is the basis of legitimacy and status for the profession. On the other hand, a theory base and ongoing research help the profession move beyond mere "competence." The pursuit of theory and research for professions are often associated with academic institutions, which even further enhances the prestige and legitimacy of a profession. We recognize Howe's private model of professions in this understanding of professional knowledge— knowledge and expertise as the basis of autonomy and control.

I do not want to argue about whether fundraising has reached a point where it can claim a knowledge base sufficient to position itself as a full-fledged profession in American society; most fundraisers would agree with outside "experts" that fundraising is "far from a mature profession" (Bloland and Bornstein, p. 120). I do want to contend that, no matter how well-developed fundraising skills and knowledge become, they will not address the more important issue of how fundraising is part of a philosophical and cultural tradition that must define and be the ultimate source of legitimacy for the profession—unless they are understood in a broader context. Fundraising must look to its historical roots and its public role to understand the source and foundation of its knowledge and practice. Fundraising is central to the public practice of philanthropy, and only in pursuit of public good will the profession play its proper role in society.

How can fundraising renew its historical and philosophical (and religious) roots? I believe that the concept of covenant (May, 1975) provides a helpful way in which to encourage such renewal. It is important to understand how the covenant relationship differs from the contract relationship so prevalent in our society and in professional work. The contract is episodic and ahistorical; it calls for a value-free understanding of human relations in society. The covenant offers a historical view of the way humans order their lives together. The original divine covenant extended to the whole of human history, bringing God's promise to humankind. Even without the theological connotations, a covenant forces us to take seriously the "long view," the rich web of relationships and promises (past, present, and future) that obligate us to each other. A covenant relationship is value-full; it is normative and moral by definition.

The fundraising profession suffers for its attempts to ground its knowledge base in a contractual understanding of human relationships. What passes for fundraising knowledge are the techniques and skills that keep things organized, that motivate people to give, that lead to larger and larger campaigns. This sort of knowledge is important only as it serves the public practice of philanthropy, the public goods that are embodied in institutional missions, and only if it is understood as part of the promotion of healthy relationships between institutions and their various friends and constituencies. This is the covenant-relationship that must be the context for philanthropy in America. In the philanthropic covenant, the vast gulf between donor and fundraiser (for which the contract relationship seems the only bridge) is closed through mutual respect "based on shared knowledge and purposes" (Payton, 1988, p. 65). The donor and the fundraising professional become participants in one common project, not two. In the philanthropic covenant, the fundraiser truly serves the love of humankind, and in that context, the diverse methods, skills, and motivations (the expertise) of the fundraising profession are understood as resources to be shared and employed in service of the covenant.

An example will clarify the implications of this philanthropic covenant. Major gift fundraising involves developing personal relationships with prospective donors to an institution whose resources are significant. In today's environment, huge capital campaigns and fund drives demonstrate that major gift efforts are an essential aspect of institutional fundraising. Techniques involved in major gift fundraising revolve around an effort to learn the donor's interests and an attempt to connect those interests to the institution's funding objectives and needs. Relationships between fundraisers and prospective donors may evolve over some time, or they may be episodic, depending on geographic proximity, the level of prior commitment, and so forth. It is quite often the case, however, that the fundraiser knows more about the prospective donor than vice versa.

In this particular case, I knew a great deal about the prospective donor. He was a retired businessman who had helped found a very successful company during his career. His wife had died several years before, and he cared for an adult son who was mentally disabled. He was a very religious man; in fact, he had made several large gifts to fairly conservative religious institutions in recent years. He was a graduate of the university's business school, but had shown no interest in their activities. Efforts by university fundraisers to develop a relationship with this man had been futile, except for that of one staff member who convinced the prospect to become involved in reviewing other prospective donors he may have known. In her meetings with this prospective donor, she learned more about his religious commitments and became convinced that, if he were to become involved any further with the university, it would be through the Divinity School. The dean of the Divinity School (for whom I worked) agreed to see this man. I dutifully gathered all the university background on the prospective donor and shared it with the dean. It was an intimidating story; there was no reason to believe this man would find us any more palatable than previous university representatives. In fact, if what we knew about his religious affiliations was true, our "brand" of religious scholarship might offend him.

As he approached his visit with this prospective donor, the dean discussed with me various strategies and techniques he might employ. We did not have high expectations. When the dean returned from his lunch with the prospect, he shook his head with a smile and reported that all of our worry was for naught. In the course of their conversation, the dean and this very religious businessman discovered common interests in medieval spirituality and the history of Christianity. Their discussion about religious affiliations had not focused on particular dogmas—a possible stumbling block—but on the role of religious community in their families. Our fundraising knowledge—knowledge about techniques and one-sided knowledge about the prospect—had not included his side of the story. In the course of their personal discussion about background, family, and faith, his story of history, theology, and philosophy was revealed and became the genuine core of a philanthropic relationship. An openness to sharing stories is part of what a philanthropic covenant means for the work of fundraising. If the knowledge is one-sided, only contracts will suffice to bridge the gap in the philanthropic relationship.

### How the public holds the profession accountable

What does the fundraising profession owe the public? It is a fascinating and disturbing question that must be answered by the profession as it explores its role and image in society. As Scott Cutlip (1990) tells us, "There are some 350,000 non-profit organizations employing this army of fundraisers in the competition for their piece of the charity pie. There are vast differences among these groups, but the public tends to view them as a uniform whole" (p. 60). Such broad stroke images of fundraisers raise perplexing issues both for the profession and for the public.

The second issue I want to address involves *the ways in which professional fundraisers are held accountable for their work*. This is an especially timely issue for fundraising because of the obvious tension between the philanthropic mission of fundraisers (and the organizations for which they work) and the aforementioned fact that the "currency" of their work is, quite literally, currency. This is a clash between the moral and economic objectives of fundraisers. Recent efforts by state and local governments to legislate regulation of professional fundraisers have met with a great outcry from the profession, but it seems obvious that such clashes are inevitable.

The language of stewardship is often used in fundraising circles to help characterize the fundraiser's role. The question is whether a richer understanding of stewardship—an understanding informed by the concept's biblical roots (Hall, 1982)—can offer the sort of critical perspective needed to move beyond the stewardship jargon lampooned by theologian Reinhold Niebuhr in 1930 as "mere philanthropy" (p. 555) to an understanding of mutual accountability that recognizes how service to the common good is a part of the public practice of philanthropy.

There is little in the literature about the fundraising profession that addresses the issue of mutual accountability (Payton, Rosso, and Tempel, 1991). What is written tends to focus on two isolated questions: First, how does the public hold fundraisers accountable, through legislation and regulation, for their potential and real abuses of public trust? Second, how do organizations hold fundraisers accountable for their actions in behalf of the organization? In response to the first question, the "public," through its government, has proposed a series of regulations that would place strict controls on who can raise money and how it can be done (Bush, 1991). The fundraising profession has responded to these proposed regulations by claiming that they are violations of First Amendment rights to free expression (and solicitation) that govern their work. The broad-stroke negative image of the profession encouraged by those who abuse the system should not be the basis for regulation; instead, the public should be educated about the role of fundraising in society and about how to recognize and monitor those who cheat the system. In response to the second question, the fundraising profession has treated accountability as a management, legal, and ethical question. Should there be contracts for fundraisers? How do we encourage ethical behavior within organizations? How do we manage good behavior and establish structures that monitor and encourage it?

These are not incorrect responses. They raise crucial issues for the day-to-day environment for the work of fundraisers. As such, however, they do not address the more central issue of the mutual relationship: the mutual accountability of the public and the fundraising profession. In a compelling document, entitled *Ethics and the Nation's Voluntary and Philanthropic Community: Obedience to the Unenforceable*, Independent Sector (1991), an organization devoted to research and advocacy on the nonprofit sector, states that "The concerns about lapses in ethical conduct touches every part of society. But, the public expects the highest values and ethics to be practiced *habitually* in the institutions of the charitable, nonprofit sector" (p. 5). This mutual relationship between the public and the voluntary sector is on a higher level of expectation; the public good requires public trust, and trust is a mutual relationship.

The concept of stewardship is especially helpful in explicating the idea of mutual trust and the relationship it implies. We might recall the biblical stories of stewards, the resources over which they were given responsibility, the expectations that were placed on them, and the faithful ways in which they lived out their obligations. Stewardship language is used extensively in talking about philanthropy. Americans in the late nineteenth and early twentieth centuries understood their voluntarism and service as civic stewardship (McCarthy, 1982). The concept is used to describe institutional accountability and ethics. Individual fundraisers are exhorted to grasp their roles as stewards of other's resources (Josephson, 1992). As the Independent Sector statement claims, however, "the higher calling of obedience to the unenforceable constitutes the larger expectations of stewardship. . . ." (Independent Sector, 1991, p. 10). This is the understanding of stewardship that genuinely captures the nature of mutual trust, of mutual accountability between the public and its philanthropic experts. It is not just what is expected.

In the end, what stewardship means for the philanthropic relationship involves not simply how well we tend to institutional resources or how we structure our behavior to promote faithful and responsible attitudes toward the gifts that are entrusted to us. Rather, the fundraising profession must see itself in cooperation with its various constituencies as stewards of the public good through the public practice of philanthropy. With such a challenge, stewardship and the relationships it engenders are judged by the good of the commons. Stewardship of the public good becomes the basis of mutual trust and accountability between fundraisers and their various audiences (Independent Sector, 1991). Once again, it is helpful to consider a practical example of what this stewardship of the public good means for the work of fundraisers. Let us assume that I am a fundraiser for a small social service agency, located in the suburb of a major urban area. I am interested, of course, in how I can raise more funds from area residents and businesses to support the important work of my agency. I pursue all the normal strategies to raise funds and am careful to see that all gifts to my agency are properly and responsibly used, based on the donor's wishes. I work hard to be a good steward of institutional resources and of the gifts given to the agency.

One day, a board member of my agency comes to me with an idea to apply for a large amount of money from a local foundation; in fact, this grant would be the largest ever received by my agency. He says that he has a connection to a board member of the foundation and will gladly "pull some strings" to ensure our successful application. The board member, a certified public accountant who also helps maintain the agency's financial records, agrees to help you with the budget for the grant. You read the guidelines for the foundation, which explicitly state that only a certain percentage of funds received can be used for administrative and other nondirect service purposes. You know from your agency's budget that this requirement would be nearly impossible for your agency to meet.

You call the board member to report this fact, and he exclaims at your conclusion, saying there is no reason why you can't reallocate costs and shift a large portion of your administrative costs to your program budget line and append a statement claiming that these costs are an accurate part of your educational (or direct service) programming. You stammer in reply. The man is, after all, an accountant—and a good one, you know. This apparently is a legal thing to do. Your justifications for agreeing with the board member are many: It is legal, and if legal, then certainly proper. The grant requirements are nitpicking and unfair, not recognizing how difficult it is to run a small social service agency. These grant requirements are arbitrary, and everyone else is probably looking for the same loophole. If you don't pursue the grant in this way, for your very good cause, someone else will, and why shouldn't your agency's good work be rewarded in this way? And the board member who has offered his leverage and professional help with this grant might be insulted if you refuse to participate in this creative accounting.

It is a difficult position for a fundraiser to be in. You want the best for your organization, and you want to keep board members happy. What should you do? This is a clear example of the unenforceable, to which the faithful steward must be obedient. You might go forward, buoyed by your various justifications for pursuing this money. You probably would receive the funding and become a hero(ine) in your agency. The foundation would never know about how your budgets were shifted. But what of the public good? What of mutual trust and accountability? The unenforceable demands that each of us is a steward of the public good, and the public good would not be served by our decision to participate in this deception. The ends (in this case, major funding for the good work of our agency) does not justify the means (deceiving a foundation)—even if we could get away with it. The difficult decision not to participate in this funding proposal may not make us popular with the board member, or perhaps even with agency staff, but stewardship is not simply the expected monitoring of resources as it serves private ends. It is challenging ourselves and our fellow citizens to serve the good of the commons.

## Vocation or career?

Who are these fundraisers, these philanthropic experts if you will, who have become such an integral part in the life of the voluntary sector in our society? The professional socialization of fundraisers is a critical issue for both the profession and for the public they ultimately serve. "Are people principally motivated to serve [good causes], or are they motivated by increased status and high income?" (Buchanan, 1993, p. 378). Here, once again, is the thorny issue of whether fundraising is a mission or a business.

The final abiding issue for the fundraising profession involves whether it is possible to talk about the character of fundraising professionals in a way that identifies motivations and virtues that mark these individuals in common. A recent National Society of Fundraising Executives (NSFRE) membership survey states that "The fund-raising profession is neither easily understood nor entered into automatically. Individuals largely discover the profession through venues other than upbringing or schooling. Few children readily contemplate fund-raising as a career" (NSFRE, 1992, p. 5). This claim may be seen as a badge of honor for the profession, but I worry that upbringing and schooling may not have a role in an individual's choice to become a professional fundraiser. That excludes some important influences. The concept of a profession as a vocation, defined as the purpose and motivation for someone's work, may serve an important role in bringing order and common direction to understanding the character of professional fundraisers.

It is instructive to begin with a "realistic" picture of the motivations of fundraisers, based on a survey of over 750 professional fundraisers conducted by Robert Carbone (1989). Carbone found that the chief motivation and priority for fundraisers is their personal success. Responses ranged from how personal success is a natural inclination of the "goal oriented" and entrepreneurial individuals who become fundraisers, to the claim that fundraisers are "like" other professionals, concerned about themselves and their families above all. Fundraisers surveyed claimed that because "society values success' and the 'money you make' . . . fundraisers merely 'reflect the values of the society in which we live'" (p. 36).

On the other hand, many fundraising professionals maintain that their overriding allegiance is to their employing organizations. They feel that they must "believe" in their organization and mission to be effective in raising money for the organizational cause. This is both an emotional and an intellectual choice. Fundraisers must 'feel' an emotional tie to the organization and must 'choose' to work for a cause in which they have an interest or commitment (Buchanan, 1993).

A third group of professional fundraisers—a minority group, according to Carbone—states that their top priority and allegiance is to fundraising as a field of work. This priority involves a mixed set of motivations, including pride, altruism, fascination with the work, and even personal commitment to the art and craft involved in fundraising.

This "realistic" picture of the priorities and motivations of professional fundraisers points to a disturbing, though understandable, contradiction and inconsistency in the profession. Fundraising *is* a job for even the most dedicated and public-minded of its practitioners. At the same time, the context and purpose of the profession is always in service of some cause (whether the individual practitioner sees that cause as crucial or not). Is it possible to hope for any better than a more balanced understanding of how self-interest and altruism work together to motivate the fundraising professional? Might we begin to set this "realistic" picture of professional fundraisers' motivations in the broader context of the public practice of philanthropy and the genuine good it serves?

I believe that we do the fundraising profession a disservice if we are not able to argue for the intrinsically moral and public role of the profession. It is not good enough to maintain a healthy balance between self-interest and altruism. To this challenge, the concept of vocation provides a corrective framework as a means of challenging the "realistic" picture of professional motivations and priorities among fundraisers. The concept of vocation reminds us that professional work must be seen as a moral commitment, defined by its broader ends and motivations (Gustafson, 1982).

What are the ends that fundraising as a vocation must serve? In a discussion of why fundraising and philanthropy lack acceptance as "professions" according to the sociological definition, Robert Payton (1988) points out that a major problem is that they pursue "ambiguous ends" (p. 83). Fundraising does not seem to have clear and commonly accepted purposes and objectives. Witness the range of priorities offered in our survey results discussed above. Instead of a clear purpose like promoting health or justice, fundraising serves the historical tradition of philanthropy and seeks to promote the public goods supported by that tradition. And, as Payton so clearly tells us, this tradition is subject to "attenuation by neglect as well as erosion by criticism" (p. 83). Historical traditions are pluralistic, embroiled in conflicts of value and purposes. Certainly any review of the historical moments in fundraising and philanthropy hint at those conflicts. In the same way, the public good as an end to be served by fundraisers is not written in stone or in the natural order of things (at least not as far as most Americans are concerned). The tradition and values reflected in the public practice of philanthropy is not some monolithic set of principles. Instead, the meaning of philanthropy and the public goods it serves must be pursued, and approximations of its central values and goals must be tested and debated in public forums. Pursuit of the public good is a process, not a given.

With these ambiguous ends as the basis for a vocational understanding of fundraising, it is little wonder that we find such lack of consistency in the motivations and priorities of fundraisers. That, however, is precisely why the concept of vocation is central to renewing a moral understanding of fundraising as a profession. The language of vocation calls to judgment anything less than a willingness to struggle with the ambiguous ends of our work. As sincere as individual fundraisers may be in their priorities, whether focused on personal success, organizational cause, or the profession itself, their attention must be directed to the philanthropic tradition and public good they are ultimately called to serve. As Martin E. Marty challenges us (with specific reference to the social work profession), "where we do not possess the traditions, they may 'still possess us,' and deserve to be kept alive as a kind of repository of options" (1980, p. 479). Fundraising must be possessed by its ambiguous ends.

What practical ways are available to the fundraising profession to keep alive its defining traditions and its service to the public good as the chief ends to be pursued? How is it possible to promote a vocational understanding of fundraising? The fundraising profession does not have the systematized professional education through which other professions can mandate a core curriculum, an accepted body of knowledge and skills, and the pursuit of professional formation. Though the number of graduate degree programs in philanthropy and fundraising have grown during the past decade (which is one sign that the 'profession' is gaining legitimacy in society), there is still little consensus about the value and utility of formal professional training for fundraisers (Buchanan, 1993, p. 375). The issue of professional socialization and formation is left to less-structured and rigorous professional development programs (like those offered by a professional association) and to the mentor relationships between senior fundraisers and those in their charge. The process by which "new" professionals are socialized into the fundraising profession—the means by which they selectively acquire the values and attitudes, and learn the culture, of fundraising—is left to senior professionals who, as we have seen in our survey of fundraising professionals above, have differing opinions about the motivations, priorities, and purposes of fundraising.

I will use myself as an example of the senior professional charged with mentoring new professionals into a responsible understanding of how their work serves the philanthropic tradition and the public good. I hired a young woman for an entry-level position in the development office that I directed several years ago. She had all the raw skills needed to succeed. She was bright, articulate, ambitious, and even socially committed. She also was a handful to supervise, both in her work and in her ongoing formation as a professional. She challenged my opinions; she insinuated herself into projects where she did not belong; she often complained that she was not getting the respect and status she deserved within the institution. When she went to a faculty member for information about the grant she was working on, she expected to be treated as a colleague. When she was not, she wanted to know why. I tried to convince her that development officers are servants of institutional missions, which in this case conferred status on the faculty members and not on her. We discussed stewardship and how it meant slavery in its biblical sense, and I asked her to reflect on what that might mean for her work. I reasoned with her about her age and relative lack of experience, and how that might be perceived by others in the institution. I appealed to her sense of the common good and to her commitments to build a more just and equitable society. I even entreated her to learn from these people's attitudes toward her so that she could model a more democratic and fair style in her own career. It was a constant battle, which I had difficulty fitting into my workload. I stayed with her because it was important; but many busy senior professionals would not stay with such a person. She learned incrementally about the role of fundraisers in organizations and in society; today she is doing well in her career, combining her enthusiasm, knowledge, skills, and moral commitments with a more tempered sense of her work's purpose. If people like me are the front lines for professional formation and socialization that takes seriously the *vocation* of fundraising and the higher purposes served by fundraising professionals, then we have to be realistic about the limits of human patience and endurance in the pursuit of the 'ambiguous ends' we serve. That, of course, does not even address the many senior professionals for whom the vocational understanding of fundraising makes little sense.

If Robert Payton is on the right track when he claims that, within the philanthropic tradition, "the moral agenda of society is put forward. . . ." (1988, p. 119) and challenges philanthropy to embrace its role as public conscience and critic (even for itself), then fundraisers—our philanthropic experts—must be formed and educated to grasp their crucial roles. The profession and the public must seek the means to make such vocational formation possible.

This chapter simply sketches the possibility of understanding fundraising as a form of public service and the implications such an understanding of the profession might have for our work. If we are to take the moral meaning of our work seriously, we must engage each other and the wider public in a conversation about how the public practice of philanthropy remains a central tenet of a democratic society. In our participation and leadership in that conversation, we illustrate the meaning of good citizenship, perhaps the highest calling for the professional in the body politic.

## References

Bellah, R. N., and Sullivan, W. M. "The Professions and the Common Good: Vocation/Profession/Career." *Religion and Intellectual Life*, 1987, *4* (3), 7–20.

Bloland, H. G., and Bornstein, R. "Fundraising in Transition: Strategies for Professionalization." In D. F. Burlingame and L. J. Hulse (eds.), *Taking Fundraising Seriously*. San Francisco: Jossey-Bass, 1991.

Buchanan, P. M. "Educational Fundraising as a Profession." In M. J. Worth (ed.), *Educational Fundraising: Principles and Practices*. Phoenix, Ariz.: American Council on Education and The Oryx Press, 1993.

Bush, B. H. "What Fundraisers Should Know About the Law." In D. F. Burlingame and L. J. Hulse (eds.), *Taking Fundraising Seriously*. San Francisco: Jossey-Bass, 1991.

Carbone, R. *Fundraising as a Profession*. College Park, Md.: Clearinghouse for Research on Fundraising, 1989.

Cutlip, S. M. *Fundraising in the United States: Its Role in America's Philanthropy*. New Brunswick, N.J.: Rutgers University Press, 1965.

Cutlip, S. M. "Fundraising in the United States." *Society*, March/April 1990, pp. 59–62.

Gustafson, J. M. "Professions as 'Callings'." *Social Service Review*, 1982, *56*, 503–515.

Hall, D. J. *The Steward: A Biblical Symbol Comes of Age*. New York: Friendship Press, 1982.

Howe, E. "Public Professions and the Private Model of Professionalism." *Social Work*, 1980, *25* (5), 179–191.

Independent Sector. *Ethics and the Nation's Voluntary and Philanthropic Community: Obedience to the Unenforceable*. Washington, D.C.: Independent Sector, 1991.

Jennings, B., Callahan, D., and Wolf, S. M. "The Professions: Public Interest and Common Good." *The Hastings Center Report*, Feb. 1987, pp. 3–10.

Josephson, M. *Ethics in Grantmaking and Grantseeking*. Marina del Rey, Calif.: The Josephson Institute, 1992.

McCarthy, K. D. *Noblesse Oblige: Charity and Cultural Philanthropy in Chicago, 1849–1929.* Chicago: University of Chicago Press, 1982.

McCollough, T. E. *The Moral Imagination and Public Life: Raising the Ethical Question.* Chatham, N.J.: Chatham House, 1991.

Marty, M. E. "Social Service: Godly and Godless." *Social Service Review,* Dec. 1980, pp. 479–495.

May, W. F. "Code, Covenant, Contract, or Philanthropy." *The Hastings Center Report.* Dec. 1975, pp. 29–38.

National Society of Fundraising Executives (NSFRE). *Profile: 1992 Membership Survey.* Alexandria, Va.: NSFRE, 1992.

Niebuhr, R. "Is Stewardship Ethical?" *Christian Century,* Apr. 30, 1930, pp. 555–557.

Payton, R. *Philanthropy: Voluntary Action for the Public Good.* New York: American Council on Education and Macmillan, 1988.

Payton, R. L., Rosso, H. A., and Tempel, E. R. "Taking Fundraising Seriously: An Agenda." In D. F. Burlingame and L. J. Hulse (eds.), *Taking Fundraising Seriously.* San Francisco: Jossey-Bass, 1991.

Reamer, F. G. *The Philosophical Foundations of Social Work.* New York: Columbia University Press, 1993.

Rosso, H. A. "A Philosophy of Fundraising." *The NSFRE Journal,* Spring 1992, pp. 55–57.

PAUL PRIBBENOW *is vice president for institutional advancement at the School of the Art Institute of Chicago.*

*A process guide is presented for the development professional, who must choose between the competing values presented by dilemmas that have an ethical component.*

# 4

# Decision making in ethics

## Barbara H. Marion

DECISION MAKING in ethics is not a challenge when there is a clear distinction between right and wrong, good and harm. Those choices are obvious and easy. In actuality, most ethical dilemmas present competing values, differing opinions, and varying solutions with positive and negative consequences.

The purpose of this chapter is to inspire the reader to identify the values that might play a role in decisions that have an ethical component and to plan, in advance, what process to follow when choosing between conflicting values.

Let us begin by establishing the framework within which this chapter is constructed, starting with common terms and definitions. Webster defines *ethics* as "a principle of right or good behavior; a system of moral principles or values; rules or standards of conduct governing members of a profession or a segment of society."

*Roget's Thesaurus* lists synonyms for the noun *ethics* as "principles, standards, norms, principles of conduct or behavior, principles of professional practice, morals, moral principles, code, ethical or moral code, ethical systems, behavioral norm, normative system," among others.

NEW DIRECTIONS FOR PHILANTHROPIC FUNDRAISING, NO. 6, WINTER 1994 © JOSSEY-BASS PUBLISHERS

Peter Drucker (1990, p. 35) maintains that ethics deals with the right actions of individuals. Michael O'Neill (1992) of the Institute for Nonprofit Management, University of San Francisco, believes that "ethics is about what human beings do when they are acting as human beings, that is with a certain amount of freedom and understanding." He furthers the proposition that "ethics pertains primarily to what human beings do as persons, whether as individuals or as occupants of particular social roles [development professionals] or as a communal group [a nonprofit organization]".

O'Neill cites Chester I. Barnard, former president of the Rockefeller Foundation, who argued that ethics is as natural, inescapable, and important a part of organizational life as it is of individual and communal life. Barnard (1938) continued with the thought that leadership had two dimensions: individual superiority, which is the technical aspect of leadership, and responsibility, which is the capacity of being firmly governed by moral codes in the presence of strong contrary impulses, desires, or interests.

Robert L. Payton, Henry A. Rosso, and Eugene R. Tempel (1991, p. 9) accept the useful distinction between morals as having to do with behavior, and ethics as systematic reflection on that behavior.

Edward Stevens (1974) argued that moral values are in a class apart. They are the test to which the morally good man submits his other values. A moral value is one that is in harmony with what it means to be a human being.

## Tiered values as a possible view

This chapter is based on the theory that moral values are the primary, unvarying bedrock rules of individual conduct that result from culture, experience, and training. They are unconditional, forming the life philosophy of the individual, the primary template against which other, second-tier values are held. Moral values can include such constants as religious imperatives and the primacy of family. Second-tier values are those that we consciously and deliberately take to form our personal code of honor based on principles such as truth-telling, love of country, respect for others, protection of the weak, and tolerance. Second-tier values, in turn, form a template for judging our third-tier values, the standards of professional practice by which we perform our duties as development practitioners.

It is on these third-tier values, the values between which choices must be made and upon which courses of action must be determined that this chapter is focused. In order to choose freely and knowingly, one must understand the alternatives. A little background in values and how they apply to development professionals may help.

## *Values in fundraising*

Psychologist Louis Edward Raths (Stevens, 1974, p. 14) formulated this seven-step valuing process to determine true values. First, a true value is something you prize and cherish. Second, you must be willing, when appropriate, to publicly affirm what you value. Third, there must be available alternatives. Fourth, a true value is chosen intelligently, after consideration of the consequences. Fifth, a value is something chosen freely, after consideration of the consequences. Sixth, a true value involves acting on your belief. Seventh, a true value involves acting on it repeatedly and with a consistent pattern.

The Josephson Institute for the Advancement of Ethics (Josephson, 1988) has proposed that a study of history, philosophy, and religion reveals a consensus as to certain core ethical values which have transcended culture and time to establish the ethical norms and standards of moral conduct essential to an ethical life. The values identified by the Institute, which provided the basis of decision making about ethical issues, are:

1. Honesty
2. Integrity
3. Promise-keeping
4. Fidelity/loyalty
5. Fairness
6. Caring for others
7. Respect for others
8. Responsible citizenship
9. Pursuit of excellence
10. Accountability

Josephson added an eleventh value for nonprofit organizations and their fundraising development professionals: safeguarding the public trust.

___

## Everyday application of values

If we take Josephson's list of ten (second tier), plus safeguarding the public trust (third tier), and suggest how they affect the decision process within the development profession, some very real, everyday issues spring to mind.

*Honesty.* The value of honesty affects such things as communications with donors, funders, and institutions. Fundraisers should be open, honest, and clear, avoiding exaggerated claims of performance and misleading descriptions of activities. Proposals should be forthright about the organization's capability, about who else is involved in the work or in the funding, and about how much was raised. The recruitment process should avoid misleading potential volunteers as to their role and the expectation that the board members will be responsible for fundraising. Development staff should avoid ingratiating themselves with a donor through false friendship, making exaggerated claims of professional experience, taking credit for the work or ideas of others, or shifting blame onto others.

*Integrity.* The value of integrity affects such things as bending the institution's mission to get funding; allowing program activities to drag the organization away from its mission; "looking the other way" at bad policies or questionable tactics.

*Promise-keeping.* The value of promise-keeping affects such things as failing to live by the spirit of the terms of a gift; misusing restricted funds or continuing to use restricted funds after the purpose has been met or the project finished; or using the precise terms of an agreement to be rigid instead of fair.

*Fidelity/loyalty.* The value of fidelity in development affects such things as violating the confidentiality of the donor or of the organization; dealing with conflicts of interest; putting personal interest above organizational interest, and organizational interest above mission interest.

*Fairness.* Josephson suggests that another word for the value of fairness is justice. The value of fairness in development affects such things as manipulating prospects or donors who are vulnerable; being overly demanding of the time of staff; exploiting donors; seeing them as lonely people who can be reached by professional "friends"; making exceptions for major donors that would not be made for others.

*Caring for others.* According to Josephson, avoiding harm is the linchpin of the application of ethical values. Often, the ethical dilemma is not avoiding harm but choosing between who will be harmed or who will be harmed the most.

*Respect for others.* The value of respect requires honoring the motivation of donors. Many, if not most, donors are interested in solutions to society's problems. Respect requires candor about the need and the manner in which the organization's program will or will not solve the problem. Respect means being cautious about how prospect and donor research is done; being diligent about how information on clients and donors is protected; cherishing the time and energy expended by volunteers; giving volunteers a clear indication of their role and responsibility before recruiting them. Respect means giving equal access to all: to donors, to service beneficiaries, to volunteers, and to staff.

*Responsible citizenship.* The value of citizenship requires adherence to all laws, social consciousness, and public service. Good citizenship includes living up to the rules of conduct for the profession and adhering to the code of ethics of your professional organization.

*Pursuit of excellence.* The value of excellence includes concern with the quality of one's own work, diligence, reliability, industry, and commitment to do one's best. It also requires instilling within each board member the importance of the mission, goals, and the role of leadership in achieving them, as well as integrating each member of the board into a productive and functioning team. Along with that is a requirement for advocacy, a show of commitment to excellence, and a display of belief in the organization. Excellence means recognizing the areas in which you are less strong and working to strengthen those areas so that you can meet your commitment to the organization and its mission.

*Accountability.* The value of accountability includes acceptance of responsibility for decisions and the consequences of actions or inaction. It requires alerting the appropriate people to a problem; fully divulging how funding was used, including fundraising and administrative costs; being a scrupulous steward over contributed dollars; confronting issues, even difficult ones, directly and quickly; planning for the future of the organization; laying the groundwork to meet future goals by projecting future demands and cultivating future support.

*Safeguarding the public trust.* According to Josephson, this includes the special obligation to lead by example, to safeguard and advance the integrity and reputation of those organizations that depend on voluntary support, and to avoid even the appearance of impropriety or self-dealing.

*Duty.* This is my suggestion for a twelfth ethical value for development professionals. Much thought has gone into suggesting a development professional's hierarchy of loyalty, which sequentially prioritizes philanthropy, donors, organization, profession, and self. My definition of the role of a development professional is to facilitate the transfer of available dollars from a willing donor to a worthy cause. I believe development professionals have a special duty to donors, a duty to act in the best interests of the donor, a duty to act as advocate for the donor. It means we have a duty to give information that allows an informed decision, a duty to ensure that the legitimate interests of the donor are protected, a duty to avoid manipulation or intimidation, and a duty to seek funds only for worthy organizations.

When a gift is unencumbered, when the furthering of mission is the value sought by the donor, fairness requires that duty to donors take precedence over duty to organization. Development professionals are skilled in the art of making compelling cases for support of the causes they serve. They have made careers out of being persuasive. The organizations they serve have superior knowledge of the issues and facts surrounding the case and the reasonable outcomes resulting from successful solicitations. With few exceptions the donor is the outsider, the innocent (as in without knowledge or guile) player in the exchange, a financial resource that relies on the integrity of the organization (as relayed by the development professional) to fairly and truthfully state the societal need and the promised solution. Such innocence, connected, as it most often is, without expectation of material return, deserves the extra ounce of duty.

To the twelve values listed above, the practitioner must add those third-tier values that are unique to one's institution and to one's professional association. For example, an organizational value may be pluralism, decision by consensus, or refusal to accept gifts from sources incompatible with the organization's mission. Most development professional associations have as a value the avoidance of percentage fundraising.

These, together with whatever moral and religious teachings absorbed throughout our lifetime, combine to create the thicket of values by which a development professional judges his or her own behavior and the behavior of others. It also creates the list of competing values from which the practitioner must select when faced with a complex decision involving ethics.

## Conflicting values in decision making

It is within the ring of competing values that practitioners need guidelines to help them sort out which action is more ethically just. Most of us assume we know right from wrong. Questions of right and wrong are easy: do not kill; do not steal; do not cheat. So are ethical questions until the choice is between competing values and one must choose which course of action is more righteous.

Assume you are the president of the board at a shelter for the homeless. Most of the residents have been evicted from their homes. Your shelter is falling on hard times. You may have to close the shelter and displace the fifty families who would have nowhere to go unless you raise $500,000 by the end of the year. Enter a widely reputed slumlord with a possible gift of $500,000. You have it on good authority that he is running for public office in the next election. In recognition of the gift, he expects publicity about his generous and civic-minded spirit. What do you do? Take the money? Refuse the gift and evict fifty families?

Or imagine, as director of development, you received a call this morning from one of your day-care center's long-time, loyal-though-modest donors who has just learned that she is coming into some money within the next six months. She very much wants to underwrite the reading room in the day-care center. The predetermined cost for this named gift opportunity is $25,000. She is ready to make her pledge and can hardly wait to part with the money. You are fairly confident that this is a one-time gift. She has already told you that she wants to give it all away now while she is alive rather than leave anything in her will. Later you receive a call from a different prospect whom you have been cultivating for fourteen months. But it's been worth it because you know that he has the capacity to give generously and often. In reviewing the commemorative opportunities, he has decided he wants to name—and fully equip—the reading room in honor of his mother who was a reading specialist. He is prepared to write a check this afternoon for $50,000. What do you do?

Both of these are, in some measure, dilemmas of blessings, but they do raise ethical questions. To whom do you owe fidelity? What about promise keeping? What course of action will serve the greatest good? What will be the consequences of your decision? How does the mandate to do no harm play out in these scenarios?

There may not be a clear right or wrong answer, but there is an answer that is ethically better. It is in situations such as these that we need guidelines, a road map to help us decide which is the best route to take. We need to know how to make the best choice.

## Decision-making process

I am indebted to Josephson, Pastin, Freeman, and Donahue for their concepts of stakeholders and their work in developing steps for decision making, some of which are adapted for purposes of this chapter.

*Clarify the problem.* What are the driving forces in the situation? Where is the pressure originating? Are the sources of the pressure reliable or may the pressure be without merit? Upon whom is the pressure being put? Given the options, what course of action will send the pressure in what direction? Are there directions in which the damage would be intolerable? Identify the specifics of the predicament. Bring it down to its essence. Remove all extraneous issues from consideration. Remove as much emotion as possible. Identify the number of players affected. Remove personalities, yours and others', from consideration; use position titles: Donor A, Staff Member D, Board Member B, and so on. Identify the critical facts of the situation and the issues at hand. Write them down—not the rumors, but the facts. Review them. Have someone else review the facts for or with you. What else do you need to know? How serious is the issue?

*Identify the key, competing values at stake.* Is this an issue of honesty, of respect, of justice, of accountability, of fairness, or all of these? Rank the values in priority order by importance and impact.

Rarely do all merit the same weight. Identify the organization's values and policies pertinent to the decision. Is there an existing policy? Does it cover the problem? Is the policy current and compatible with the organization's stated values? How many different policies and values are pertinent to the issue? Do any take precedence over others?

*Identify the players and stakeholders.* Who should have a role in making the decision? Does the dilemma involve donors, clients, staff, the community, volunteers, oneself, or philanthropy? Who is most vulnerable? Are there stakeholders who merit more protection than others? Try to rank these in priority by the weight of their value in the dilemma and the relative negative impact on each stakeholder.

*Identify the most plausible alternatives.* Plot the differing solutions that could resolve the problem. Note the values, policies, and players affected by each solution.

*Imagine the potential outcomes.* For each alternative solution, imagine the probable outcomes, both positive and negative. What are the short-term effects? What are the long-term implications? What is the worst-case scenario? Note the effect each outcome has on the players or stakeholders as well as on the organization's mission. Are there stakeholders who would be more damaged? How would justice, or lack of justice, affect each stakeholder?

*Evaluate the potential outcomes.* Rank the potential outcomes according to the positive and negative results, the harm or good each would cause, the number of players affected, the short-term effects, and the long-term implications.

*Decide on a course of action.* Take all of the information on balance. Take your time and allow all facets of the dilemma to come into view. Try to back your own emotions and prejudices out of the process. Think, read, roll it over in your mind. If it is not an emergency, sleep on it a few days; problems tend to show other dimensions over time, and the mind often finds solutions when at rest. Select from the alternatives the course of action that is ethically better, the alternative that is least damaging, more in concert with higher tier values. Write down your decision. Have a clear understanding of why you believe this is the best course of action.

*Test the decision.* James Donahue (1988) of Georgetown University's Department of Theology suggests that the decision be tested for the following:

*Consistency:* Is this decision consistent with previous actions for which the organization, or the person, have become known? Does the decision fit with the organization's history? Would you apply the same principles to future actions?

*Coherence:* Is this decision in line with the decisions of other segments of the organization? Do different parts of the organization reflect a unified decision-making process?

*Communication:* Has the discussion that led to the decision been open and candid? Have all the right people been involved in the decision?

*Conviction:* Is the decision consistent with the mission and purposes of the organization? Does the decision reflect the values of the organization's culture?

*Creativity:* Does the decision take sufficient account of new ideas and discoveries that might lead to new advances and rewards for the organization, for society?

*Share the decision with someone else.* Ethical decisions that affect organizations are best when they are shared, preferably within the organization. However, if you feel that you are more right than the others grappling with the dilemma, remember Barnard's view (1938) that we need to continually strengthen our "capacity of being firmly governed by moral codes in the presence of strong contrary impulses, desires, or interests."

*Implement the decision.* While implementing, try to minimize the negative impacts on the various stakeholders; when possible make them privy to the procedure that resulted in the decision, the evidence of concern for their rights and comfort, and the equity of the decision.

*Evaluate the results or consequences.* After closure, when all the results are known, evaluate the consequences and results of the decision. Also evaluate the process that led to the decision. Identify weaknesses and strengths within the procedure.

*Modify policies and procedures.* Develop or modify any policies or procedures found to be lacking in the course of evaluating the decision-making process.

## When third-tier values conflict with first- or second-tier values

Occasionally, development professionals will find themselves in situations where the organization being served develops values that are in conflict with the practitioner's code of professional ethics. Such situations call for discussion, education, and persuasion as to the better course of action. Not every deviation from code or every failure to persuade must result in resigning in protest. Some of these situations may be the result of honest disagreements or varying professional standards. They may be resolved by agreeing to disagree and putting the disagreement on the record. As Hank Goldstein says, not every ethical conflict requires the professional "to fall on his sword."

When should you consider the possibility of seeking other employment? Perhaps repeated scenarios that compromise your third-tier values, such as accountability or duty-to-donors. What should compel you to resign without hesitation is any situation that requires you to violate your second- or first-tier values, the bedrock unconditional beliefs that define you as the human you are. The very essence of philanthropy is based on the values of humanity. Our profession should not require the compromise of our life values.

### References
Barnard, C. I. *The Functions of the Executive.* Cambridge, Mass.: Harvard University Press, 1938.

Donahue, J. "Ethics in the Fundraising Decision-Making Process." Paper presented at National Society of Fund Raising Executives, International Conference, Nashville, Tenn., 1988.

Drucker, P. F. *Managing the Non-Profit Organization: Practices and Principles.* New York: HarperCollins, 1990.

Freeman, R. E. *Strategic Management: A Stakeholder Approach.* Boston: Pitman, 1984.

Josephson, M. "Ethical Obligations and Opportunities in Philanthropy and Fundraising." Paper presented at the National Forum on Fund-Raising Ethics, National Society of Fund Raising Executives, Alexandria, Va., Dec. 11–13, 1988.

O'Neill, M. "Ethical Dimensions of Nonprofit Administration." *Nonprofit Management & Leadership,* 1992, *3* (2), 199–213.

Pastin, M. *The Hard Problems of Management: Gaining the Ethics Edge.* San Francisco: Jossey-Bass, 1986.

Pastin, M. "The Ethics Imperative." *Planning Forum.* Oxford, Ohio: Network Publications, 1992.

Payton, R. L., Rosso, H. A., and Tempel, E. R. "Toward a Philosophy of Fund Raising." In D. F. Burlingame and L. J. Hulse (eds.), *Taking Fundraising Seriously.* San Francisco: Jossey-Bass, 1991.

Raths and Associates. *Values and Teaching.* Columbus, Ohio: Merrill, 1966.

Stevens, E. *The Morals Game.* New York: Paulist Press, 1974.

BARBARA H. MARION *is principal of Marion Fundraising Counsel, San Francisco; adjunct faculty member at the College of Professional Studies, University of San Francisco; former chair of the National Society of Fund Raising Executives (NSFRE); and longtime member of the NSFRE Ethics Committee.*

*Board members of nonprofit organizations have a significant role in setting an ethical tone and applying ethical decision making in the fundraising practices of nonprofit organizations.*

# 5

## Ethics and the nonprofit board of directors

*Jane C. Geever*

IT IS HARD for the average person to determine what is the right answer—what is the correct decision—what is ethical. For many of us, behaving ethically means that we feel right about what we do because of what we have learned during our lifetime. We behave ethically because of what we believe.

When we take on a *leadership* role as a board member of a nonprofit organization, we will often be called upon to make decisions in an arena that may be unfamiliar to us. What do we do? We need to rely on our well-developed intuitive skills. But we also need to go one step further. We should help our nonprofit agency develop a mechanism, a process for ethical decision making. Basically, we would be helping our nonprofit experience the same ethical decision-making learning curve that we personally experienced. The end product within our nonprofit should be a way of thinking that influences ethical behavior.

Ethical decision making is often elusive. In the nonprofit setting, when fundraising is the issue, it becomes especially difficult. The lifeblood of fundraising—securing donations—can cause board and

NEW DIRECTIONS FOR PHILANTHROPIC FUNDRAISING, NO. 6, WINTER 1994 © JOSSEY-BASS PUBLISHERS

staff alike to set aside ethical considerations in favor of short-term, pragmatic decisions.

In a survey of current research about fundraising, Virginia A. Hodgkinson notes: "It is clear that if a charity engages in fraudulent or unethical practices, it will lose the public trust and thus contributions" (1989, p. 7). This fact should give a nonprofit's board good reason to examine closely its ethical priorities.

---

## Elusive nature of ethical decision making

Nonprofit decision makers rarely confront black and white choices, especially when fundraising issues are at question. The pressure of financial survival may lead to shortcuts that are ethically questionable.

Amar Bhide and Howard Stevenson (1990) remind us that "There is no compelling reason to tell the truth" (p. 121). In their survey of business leaders, they found that most believed in keeping their promises because it is ethical, not because it is wise business practice. They state: "The importance of moral and social motives in business cannot be overemphasized . . . we keep promises because we believe it is right to do so—not because it is good business" (p. 128).

If ethics in the corporate world is based on "soft" rationale, when ethics is coupled with nonprofit fundraising practice, it becomes all the more tricky. As Paul Ylvisaker (unpublished manuscript, 1982) said, "When you put two words like ethics and philanthropy together, you are in trouble; each of them resists definition, and when combined, they can be totally elusive."

The nonprofit world is viewed differently than are the worlds of business and government. A special trust is vested in nonprofits due to the nature of the work performed by its members. The business of the nonprofit "embodies a nobility that exceeds the purposes of government and business" (Fogal, 1991, p. 263).

That trust puts pressure on nonprofits to behave in an ethical manner. When that doesn't happen, the public reaction far outweighs the seriousness of the offense. We have witnessed public outrage at the behavior and decisions of such nonprofit leaders as Reverend Jim Bakker, Father Bruce Ritter, and William Aramony.

The Independent Sector (IS) report, *Ethics and the Nation's Voluntary and Philanthropic Community*, notes: "People put faith in us just because we are supposed to be charitable" (1991, p. 9), and "Those who presume to serve the public good must assume a public trust" (p. 1).

Independent Sector reminds us that in all decision making we must go beyond the law and even the spirit of the law. "The essential test of ethical behavior is 'obedience to the unenforceable,' originally described by England's Lord Justice of Appeal John Fletcher Moulton 65 years ago as obedience to self-imposed law" (p. 3).

It is the volunteer board leaders who must create the desire for and model such behavior within nonprofits, especially behavior related to fundraising practice.

---

## Setting an ethical tone for fundraising within a nonprofit agency

Peter Bell's (1993) thoughts on this issue are worth noting: "If America's non-profits are to preserve their independence, they must maintain the public trust that is essential to their work. The responsibility for re-affirming that trust lies with those responsible for governing the non-profit world: members of charity and foundation boards. . . . This concept of trusteeship allows the citizens who serve on non-profit boards to shape organizations in accord with their diverse values and ideas. It also builds on the assumption that board members will exercise their responsibility in pursuit of the public good" (p. 40).

As Robert Fogal (1991) notes, "how a nonprofit conducts fundraising says a great deal about and may actually determine the organization's character" (p. 264). Fundraising policies and practices demonstrate a nonprofit's commitment to its public purpose. Board members' values and attitudes are manifested in their organizations' fundraising; the driver for ethical behavior has to be the board.

Through its governance function, the board sets the tone for all of a nonprofit's decision making.

The Independent Sector report (1991) quoted previously points out the board's importance in promoting strong ethical behavior in a nonprofit: "The ethical behavior of an institution is the ultimate responsibility of its trustees" (p. 7). And, "the basic means by which we can ensure confidence in philanthropic and voluntary organizations is to demonstrate the quality of our leadership. This demonstration begins with full and consistent evidence that trustees, staff directors and all other participants reflect habitually the ethics people have a right to expect of them and they make ethical practices part of the organization's culture" (p. 10).

Just as the board is expected to provide leadership in all other areas of a nonprofit's management, they must do so on issues of ethics. But how? How do a lawyer, a fireman, a volunteer, and a public relations executive develop a set of shared values that can then be imbued into the organizational policies of a nonprofit agency? Kenneth R. Andrews suggests: "Ethical decisions depend on both the decision-making process itself and on the experience, intelligence, and integrity of the decision maker" (1989, p. 100). Christine Milliken adds: "Given the diversity of the sector, legal standards and rules are not enough. Voluntary standards and guidelines of good practices play an important role. The very process of creating them forces the airing of questions and issues that might otherwise be avoided. They also serve as an educational tool for new board members and for the public at large" (1988, p. 31).

Establishing a process and imbuing everyone within an organization with an awareness of the importance of ethical decision making are critical first steps that must be initiated by the board.

Independent Sector released a statement in 1991 on the issue of ethical behavior in nonprofits. The statement was the culmination of eighteen months of deliberation by a task force of thirty individuals, including this author, representing all aspects of the Third Sector. The following reflects the steps suggested in the IS report, *Ethics and the Nation's Voluntary and Philanthropic Community.*

*Step 1: Adopt an organizational credo.* This statement, which can be as brief as a sentence or two, should be used in the same way as a mission statement. It reflects the beliefs of the agency, is shared with all staff and clients, and is a keystone to individual behavior.

The dialogue that takes place on all levels within the agency is very important because it gets board and staff thinking on the same wavelength. A natural outcome of this first step in the process will be the discussion of ethical dilemmas with which board and staff have grappled. Thus begins the building of awareness and development of a corporate culture that encourages ethical thinking about issues, which can translate into practice.

*Step 2: Perform an annual self-evaluation.* Productive discussion about ethical behavior is now occurring on a regular basis. If this dialogue is not encouraged and if the agency does no further thinking about its ethical positions, then its ethical culture will wither away.

Central to this nurturing, then, is that board and staff take time annually to examine ethical positions. Questions such as the following should be raised: Is the credo still relevant? Does it need to be revised? Have all of the agency's legal requirements been met? Are any practices contrary to the agency's core values? What are they and how should they be changed? Are there changes in the external environment that deserve discussion because they might change agency ethical behavior?

This step is an important reaffirmation by board and staff to ethical behavior within your nonprofit.

*Step 3: Obtain an external audit.* Periodically, a trained outsider should review the credo and ethical process established by your agency. The goal of this exercise is to ensure that ethical behavior remains strong and to bring new ideas to your agency.

This exercise will add a new dimension to the discussions of board and staff. Reaffirmation of the work undertaken to date will encourage all and bring about dynamic growth.

*Step 4: Infuse these beliefs into the culture of the agency.* Robert Haas, in an interview reported in the *Harvard Business Review*, says, "Values provide a common language for aligning a company's leadership and its people" (Howard, 1990, p. 134). He goes on to explain that unless people in leadership positions model appropriate behaviors, others in the organization do not pick them up and follow them on their own.

Another way to improve ethical behavior is through training. Once ethical beliefs and behavior are thought through by the board and staff, it is critical that the board continue its leadership role beyond the discussion stage. A plan for dialogue between and training for all levels in an organization is essential. The board in its own decision making must mirror the credo and the corporate culture of ethical behavior.

*Step 5: Renew the concepts.* Utilizing the annual internal review and the periodic external audit, the board must constantly renew its belief in the importance of ethical behavior. It must exploit all positive external feedback. Sharing this information reinforces belief within the organization that ethical behavior does "pay off" and is good business.

Being an ethical board member is both a blessing and a burden; one cannot ignore the responsibility.

## Specific fundraising practices

In the first section of this chapter, it was pointed out that ethical decision making is difficult at best. But the situation is further exacerbated when the issue deals with fundraising for these reasons: there is no single set of accepted standards that guides nonprofit fundraising, and fundraising directly affects the public, which on the whole understands little about the operation of nonprofits while expecting a high standard of performance.

Boards must provide ethical guidance, therefore, on issues related to fundraising practice and to dealing with the public. A few issues deserved to be singled out for further exploration by nonprofit boards.

## Board member involvement in fundraising

Too often today, board members avoid personal involvement in fundraising on behalf of their nonprofits. They are simply unwilling to fundraise, suggesting instead that staff be hired to do the job. This contradicts an old adage in fundraising, that the most effective solicitors are volunteers. Further, one of the key functions of board members is to assist the nonprofit organizations they serve by obtaining the financial resources necessary for their operation.

While dedicated staff support, however it is provided, is critical to the success of the nonprofit's fundraising, so is the involvement of board members.

This is a practical issue for nonprofits as well as an issue of ethical practice and commitment for board members.

## Compensation

Often board members are uncomfortable with the idea of paying an agreed-upon salary to internal fundraising staff or a set fee to outside counsel. The argument offered goes something like this: "Won't they work harder if they are paid a percentage of what they raise?" or "Other professionals, such as lawyers, work for percentage compensation. Why can't fundraisers?"

The pragmatic response is, "Fine, that's a great idea." But the ethical thinker says, "Wait a minute. Don't we have a few problems here?" For example, how would a donor react, knowing part of his or her gift goes directly to the fundraiser, rather than that the fundraiser's salary is being paid out of overhead? Many donors would not approve. Also, fundraising is a relationship-building business. If a gift is solicited prematurely, the result may be a smaller gift than the agency should expect, no gift at all, or even worse, permanent damage to the relationship between the organization and the donor. If a fundraiser is being paid a percentage of what is raised, or a bonus based on the total amount raised, it may be more likely that some gifts will be solicited prematurely.

The issue of compensation represents a good example of how the board can practice important ethical role-modeling. Following are some recommendations to consider regarding compensation for internal fundraising staff: (1) Provide adequate pay for experience. (2) Provide sufficient funds so a new position is covered for at least one year and ideally for two years. Staff shouldn't be hired then told, "First thing you have to do is go out and raise your salary." (3) Avoid tying compensation or bonus to results.

When retaining fundraising counsel, it is recommended that nonprofit agencies negotiate an agreed-upon set fee or reimbursement schedule and avoid tying payment to results. That means no percentage, commission, or bonus.

### Gift acceptance policy

It may be hard to believe, but not every gift given to every nonprofit should be accepted, and accepted without consideration. Here are some examples of "red flags" that should prompt discussion about a gift: (1) The purpose for which the gift is made may not be within the mission of the nonprofit or may lead to overemphasis of one program. (2) The donor may place requirements on the nonprofit that are not acceptable. (3) The manner in which the money was made or obtained by the potential donor may be objectionable.

Having a policy will prompt discussion should a gift be offered that the agency ought to question before accepting.

### Recognizing that the donor comes first

It was noted above that fundraising is relationship-building. An organization's attitude toward its donors is another basic ethical dimension that permeates an organization.

The donor should be cherished as a special friend. This means that a nonprofit should relate to the donor in the following ways: (1) by constantly sharing information, both good and bad, about the nonprofit and its services (a donor deserves to see the entire picture); (2) by getting to know the individual donor and understanding why he or she supports your nonprofit; (3) by always putting the donor first in regard to when to ask, how to ask, and what to ask for.

An ethical belief in the importance of the donor can itself dramatically change basic fundraising attitudes and practices.

## Monitoring all expenditures

Financial support is given to a nonprofit so it can maintain and expand its programs, services, research, or whatever. It is incumbent that the board set standards so that philanthropic dollars will not be wasted in unnecessary expenditures.

The board, by its own actions and decisions, sets a very important example with regard to the use of funds. If the board condones excessive expenditures, it will be extremely difficult to curb staff spending, even for the smallest items. On the other hand, if the board is appropriately frugal, the message will not be lost to all staff who control resources.

The ethical decision-making process points to the significance of prudence with regard to expenditure, as well as sufficient oversight of these expenditures by the board.

The outcry over the appearance of excessive expenditure by former United Way president William Aramony is a good lesson to all nonprofit boards about the importance of setting standards and reviewing expenditures.

## Compliance with the law

There are legal requirements that all nonprofits must follow. Some monitor the finances of the organization; others relate to its organization and operation.

An ethical responsibility of the board is to be certain that staff comply with the law and all of its ramifications. Today the board is not exempt from this responsibility by saying, "We didn't know what was going on" or "We were not advised by staff."

The board must create a process that will allow it to monitor staff activity in this crucial area.

## Educating the public

The public does not understand much about the operations of nonprofits. Studies prove that donors want information, especially about services provided, the related costs, and the cost of fundraising.

In her survey of current research about fundraising, Virginia Hodgkinson drew this conclusion: "There seems to be less consensus or knowledge about how effectively charities do their jobs, although an overwhelming proportion of the public believes charities use their donations for their intended purposes" (1989, p. 7).

Further, Christine Milliken writes: "The beginning of that process in your organization is the recognition that there is a need to educate your members and the public, not only about your program, but about how it operates, and beyond that, who you are" (1988, p. 31).

To date, nonprofits are not mandated to provide much of this information. Yet doesn't it make sense to give donors data that they can use and that might positively affect the size of the gift? Without overstepping the boundaries of its governance function, the board can encourage this vital sharing of data.

## Conclusion

Board members may question whether they are capable of being Solomon-like when it comes to setting the ethical standards and monitoring the ethical practice of their nonprofit's fundraising effort. As difficult as it may be for the individual, Bell underscores how important any and all effort is when he reminds us that "The real cost—difficult to measure, but still great—is the good that goes undone" (1993, p. 41).

Take to heart the ideas and thoughts presented here. Develop a plan to adopt them. Get input and feedback from other key board members. Remember that change comes slowly, but if you continue your efforts, change will result.

### References

Andrews, K. R. "Ethics in Practice." *Harvard Business Review*, Sept.–Oct. 1989, pp. 99–104.

Bell, P. D. "Boards Must Rebuild Public Trust in Charities." *The Chronicle of Philanthropy*, Nov. 30, 1993, pp. 40–41.

Bhide, A., and Stevenson, H. H. "Why Be Honest If Honesty Doesn't Pay." *Harvard Business Review*, Sept.–Oct. 1990, pp. 121–129.

Fogal, R. E. "Standards and Ethics in Fund Raising." In H. A. Rosso and Associates (eds.), *Achieving Excellence in Fund Raising: A Comprehensive Guide to Principles, Strategies, and Methods.* San Francisco: Jossey-Bass, 1991.

Hodgkinson, V. A. *What We Know About Public Attitudes Toward Charitable Organizations.* Unpublished manuscript, May 1989.

Howard, R. "Values Make the Company: An Interview with Robert Haas." *Harvard Business Review,* Sept.–Oct. 1990, pp. 133–144.

Independent Sector. *Ethics and the Nation's Voluntary and Philanthropic Community: Obedience to the Unenforceable.* Washington, D.C.: Independent Sector, 1991.

Milliken, C. "What Should the Nonprofit Sector Stand For? Ethics, Values and Standards" (Part 3). *Donor Briefing,* Feb. 17, 1988, *3* (4), 25–31.

JANE C. GEEVER *is president of J. C. Geever, Inc., a fundraising consulting firm that she founded in 1975. She lectures widely and has several published works related to grantsmanship and philanthropy.*

*Executive Search, unlike other professional services, is not regulated; therefore, ethical behavior is defined by its own practitioners. Although complex and subjective, guidelines do exist.*

# 6

# Ethical dilemmas of retained search for nonprofit organizations

*Janis M. Zivic*

MORE THAN EVER before, the fundraising/nonprofit community has begun to look to professional search consultants to help it find solutions to staffing needs, historically marred by rapid turnover. Since fundraising offers new opportunities for business, search companies welcome the philanthropic "industry." In order to leverage the search process, however, fundraisers must address key ethical issues.

In discussing the search process, I refer only to retained search (not contingency). In working with a contingency firm, the client organization pays a predetermined fee to the consultant who represents the candidate hired. The fee is "contingent" upon hire. In a retainer agreement, the client pays a fee (or retainer) for completion of a search process or project; the final payment is not determined by (or contingent upon) a placement or hire. It is clear to everyone, however, that in most retained search assignments, someone is hired or "placed"; otherwise the search consultant would acquire a reputation for incomplete or unsuccessful assignments. The industry is far too competitive for such results to be acceptable.

NEW DIRECTIONS FOR PHILANTHROPIC FUNDRAISING, NO. 6, WINTER 1994 © JOSSEY-BASS PUBLISHERS

## *What is fair billing practice?*

The standard retainer fee for executive search firms ranges from 30 percent to 40 percent of the first year's cash compensation paid to the final or hired candidate, plus out-of-pocket expenses generated during the search process. Many search firms will not negotiate their stated fee. In fact, consultants often believe it is unethical for the search firm to negotiate a fee when the sole purpose of the negotiation is to garner business. However, as fees do fluctuate between firms and within certain industries, options nonprofits may consider when negotiating retainer fees for development assignments are noted here. Though not intended to be comprehensive, this list introduces several options that fall within ethical guidelines of the practice.

*Volume discounts.* If a firm is retained to complete more than one assignment simultaneously, a "volume discount" is commonly available and is rarely viewed as an unethical negotiation.

*Fixed fee arrangements.* "Fixed Fee" arrangements, in which both the client and the search consultant share a risk, are becoming more common. As an example, for a search estimated to be in the $60,000 to $90,000 compensation range, the fee is "fixed" at $25,000, 33⅓ percent of the mid-point, $75,000. If the search firm's standard fee is 33⅓ percent and the candidate is hired at the top end of the range or higher, the search firm has given up $5,000 or more. If the candidate is hired at $60,000, the client has paid a premium of $5,000. My experience suggests that, as a rule, nonprofit clients tend to underestimate the salary necessary to recruit the new employee, and search consultants are adjusting their fixed fees accordingly.

*Out-of-pocket expenses.* For years professional service firms summarized expenses and were rarely asked to isolate the details of the expenditures. Today "billable hours" and "indirect cost" policies have caused crises in financial management. The search industry has not gone unnoticed in this analysis.

Out-of-pocket expenses are controllable. The client should understand exactly what the monthly billings for expenses include. Many firms will agree to place a ceiling on their expenses; anything over that amount is absorbed by the search firm. It is also possible (although not popular) for nonprofit clients to request approval for any expense over a predetermined amount *before* it is spent. Consultant travel expenses to interview candidates are commonly pre-screened, but candidate travel expenses are never negotiable.

*Pro-bono.* If a search firm offers to perform on a pro-bono basis plus expenses, it may be appropriate to question the proverbial "gift horse." Two items necessitate scrutiny: (1) Make certain the search firm clarifies its definition of the "out-of-pocket expenses," and (2) find out who will do the work. If your staffing needs provide on-the-job training for an inexperienced search associate, you may want to reconsider the advantage of a pro-bono approach.

Most search firms will perform search assignments at a reduced rate for nonprofit clients. Does this not speak to the ethics and values of the search community itself? I believe it speaks well of an industry often criticized for a lack of clear ethical structure.

---

## Should I retain a search consultant who specializes in fundraising?

Whether or not a search consultant should develop an industry or function specialization is a complex question. Reputable search firms and general practitioners of the business follow a policy referred to as the "closed client" rule, which directly affects this question.

In essence, the rule states that for a period of approximately two years after being retained, the search firm will not recruit candidates from the client organization. This "closed client" rule is clear, fundamentally, and is upheld by ethical search consultants. However, the parameters of this policy may vary when the clients are large multidivision or regionalized corporations, particularly in our global economy. For example, if a consultant has been retained by the University of California at Davis, are candidates from the University of California at Irvine available for recruitment?

As both universities are part of the same system, search professionals will answer this question differently. Some firms have a policy stating that, if a corporation, system, or institution retains a search firm, the institution in its total is a "client" and cannot be targeted for recruitment for at least two years. Others will delineate the client's "off limit" status to boundaries defined by regions or individual incorporations. It is incumbent on the client to have the search firm clarify its policy before retaining it.

The client's dilemma is also clear. If the client wants to retain a search consultant who "specializes" in an industry or function, at what point are enough clients "closed" to the consultant that he or she is no longer able to provide a thorough "search" for the new client?

In evaluating search firms, the client should request the search firm's complete (not selected or representative) client list. Every search firm maintains one and should be willing to provide it.

It is important to note here that the search firm, not the individual search consultant, has a client list. It would be dishonest for a consultant to suggest otherwise. In most cases, the larger the firm, the longer the list. Unless you are willing to retain an individual or firm with no experience in your specific area of interest, every firm will have some "closed clients." If you want a search consultant with substantial search experience in a particular area of specialization, comparing client lists of several search firms is one part of the process that should prove helpful.

Another, and more critical, part of the process is to complete references on the consultant who will actually do the work, not the senior partner who sells the search nor the junior associate who may complete much of the initial sourcing and research. Note here that it is the individual consultant, not the search firm, who must be referenced. The firm may have completed dozens, even hundreds of development searches. The question is: how experienced and successful has this particular consultant been in the area of interest to you? The client must ask these questions since a consultant in the "sales" mode may not volunteer the limits of his experience. When possible, reference other clients who have used more than one of the consultants whose work is being evaluated.

Each search consultant has a unique combination of skills, experience, and personal characteristics that enable him or her to work more effectively in particular industries or functional areas and with particular clients. Find out who has the best reputation for working with your industry or function, or with your type of institution. Although acquiring this information takes time, it can easily be done and is critical to the success of the search process. It is often true that the ethical practices of the consultant may prove a greater influence on the success of your search than many other factors.

If the individual you are considering retaining for a search is also a management consultant, an outplacement consultant, or a dedicated fundraising consultant, the fact that their practice is not limited to "Executive Search" does not eliminate them from having "closed clients." They must be willing to define their policy for you or you run the risk, by omission, of allowing them to recruit *your* employees after you have retained them. In this situation, clarifying these boundaries may be viewed as your ethical responsibility as the client choosing the search consultant as well as the responsibility of the search firm itself.

This issue brings up another question. If you choose a consultant because he will then know you and will be able to recruit you personally for that ideal position you have been waiting for, you need to think again. If the consultant will "break the rules" for you in appreciation for all the work you have given him, when and for whom does he not break the rules?

Clients often want a search consultant who "has a Rolodex of good candidates" and can complete the search quickly. Are you paying a fee for a search of a Rolodex, or a search of an industry, or a search of the U.S.? An experienced search consultant should have a wealth of sources in the firm's computerized data base, as well as personal knowledge of the few truly extraordinary leaders in a specific arena; but if the only candidates presented to you are those who were known to the search consultant before the search was initiated, you are probably not benefitting in a manner commensurate with the fee.

## Development dilemmas

The search consultant faces several predictable dilemmas in development assignments. Although many of these dilemmas warrant their own essays, let us briefly consider three that introduce additional ethical questions.

### Incentive compensation

First is the question of incentive compensation. There is a growing trend for nonprofits to seek executives from for-profit corporations. As these senior executives are recruited for their management expertise, they expect their skills to be evaluated and their accountability to be measured. It is no surprise that performance incentives are an appropriate part of the compensation package that these executives expect when considering a new career opportunity.

NSFRE's "Standards of Professional Practice," found in the "Code of Ethical Principles" (see Conclusion, this volume) states: "Members shall work for a salary or fee, not percentage-based compensation or commission." Further, "Members may accept performance-based compensation such as bonuses provided that such bonuses are . . . not based on a percentage of philanthropic funds raised." Several issues arise.

A "management by objectives" (MBO) approach is commonly used in determining executive incentive compensation. Is it not standard for the development officer to have a stated dollar target as a goal? If the development officer is to "raise funds," isn't his performance evaluation, in part, based on the total of the funds raised?

One question often cited in this debate is understandably complex: "Who should get credit for a major gift when the development officer who orchestrated and made the ask leaves the organization before the gift is donated?"

A similar question may be asked of a corporate marketing executive. If a marketing director creates and implements an advertising campaign, only to leave his position before the campaign's success leads to a substantial increase in corporation sales, who gets "credit" for the profit increase? Would the new marketing director, who is responsible for managing the department, get the "credit" and the subsequent incentive bonus when the profit increase is applied to his "management objectives"?

How is a development officer's situation different? Once again, there is no simple solution, but the development community must realize that such issues will continue to be problematic in recruiting for-profit executives for development roles. My personal experience has proven that practice and policy are often in conflict. The compensation package for development executives often includes an "incentive bonus," an amount partially based on the total of funds raised.

Does this practice reflect negatively on the ethics of the candidate/development officer who accepts the parameters of the compensation package, the institution that creates the management objectives and consequent compensation, or the executive recruiter who negotiated the compensation? I believe the recruiting consultant's ethics are not in question in this instance. But both the development officer and the hiring nonprofit need to be clear about how the hiring practices fit the ethical standards for which they want to be recognized.

### Diversity: Gender and race

A second dilemma arises around gender and race. The majority of the highest level "Major Gifts" and advancement positions are held by white males. To be more specific, almost every Ivy League and Pac Ten University in the U.S. has a white male in the top position. My goal here is not to question the wisdom of this reality, but to acknowledge the search consultant's ethical dilemma when asked to participate in these hiring decisions.

### The law

Suppose the client, the chief development officer, cautions: "In the 100 years of our history we have never had a female or minority director; I don't believe our major donors are ready for one. Therefore, I will only interview white males for this position." The search consultant cannot, legally, accept such a search assignment where the client's definition of candidates is limited by gender (or race, age, and so on). It is a simple legal decision for the search consultant. One might ask, however, how many professionals make decisions they know to be illegal? I'm afraid I would have to answer "many." The continuance of this practice hides under the guise of the confidential "client/consultant relationship."

### A professional quandary

It becomes an ethical question when the search consultant decides whether or not to attempt to influence the client; decides whether or not to use his skill, knowledge, and experience to prove to the client that there are candidates who will be accepted by the donors and therefore will be successful; decides whether or not to present candidates to the client to demonstrate the availability and competency of candidates outside the limitations of the position requirements.

It is not enough for the consultant to refuse the search assignment with gender or race limitations. Candidates who represent diversity do exist; it is unquestionably the professional responsibility of the search consultant to influence this process, in fact, to make it work.

### Donor relationships

The recent trend for nonprofits to utilize executive search poses relevant questions involving development assignments. Historically, search consultants have "targeted" organizations where candidates may be found who possess the combined set of skills, knowledge, technology, and management style that the client is seeking. This is neither unusual nor unethical; it is the very nature of the business.

Our third dilemma is raised when the client is aware of the donors with whom another organization's Director of Major Gifts has strong relationships and therefore targets that individual as a candidate. First, is it professional for the client to pursue this Director of Major Gifts, specifically because of the relationships? Second, if this knowledge is passed on to the search consultant, is it ethical for the consultant to pursue this specific candidate based solely on knowledge of the financial capacity of particular donors the candidate has previously cultivated?

Once recruited, is it then acceptable for the director to continue to develop these same relationships for his new client/institution? These are questions for the development community and not the search industry. If it is within the ethical parameters of development to "share" major donor/development relationships, it is certainly within those for the search consultant.

There are, however, segments of this process in which the search consultant cannot participate ethically. A client should not limit the qualifications and only consider the candidate's past relationships with major donors. Nor should the client assign the responsibility to the consultant to identify the candidate's "contacts" or major donor relationships and utilize only that information for final qualification.

Considered from another point of view, is it ethical for the candidate to make his donor relationships known to the search consultant during the initial interview process so as to improve his candidate standing? This is uncommon practice during development interviews.

It is the responsibility of the search consultant to judge the appropriateness of the candidate's total experience as a fit for the client organization. In the end, the candidate's success will prove the search consultant's value to the recruiting process and to the client organization itself.

## Reference checking

Today, because of the increasingly litigious nature of our culture, many institutions have guidelines for giving references that make it impossible to complete a thorough reference check. Legally, an institution has the right to limit the reference to the employee's name, title(s) during employment, and dates of employment. If a candidate suggests that this is the only information he can make available, I will not represent the candidate. In essence, the candidate must be asked to request that his references break the institutional policy (when there is one), but this must be accomplished in order for the consultant to complete his contractual agreement with the client and obtain all relevant references.

As employment litigation evolves, search consultants have been directed by legal advisers to acquire a written agreement from the candidate that allows for reference checking without limitation to any specific institution or individual. More and more search practitioners are heeding this advice to avoid having to participate in any related candidate/employee-employer suits.

Respecting the need for confidentiality is the key to ethical behavior here. When the candidate is employed, it is imperative that the consultant and the candidate agree on referencing specific individuals. This is only a matter of clear communication between the two individuals. A final reference can be completed with the candidate's current employer after an offer has been extended "contingent upon final references."

Although it may still occur, today it is unusual for a search consultant to risk employment security for candidates. The understandable need for confidentiality is respected by all parties. Permission to complete references is given to the consultant by the candidate; thorough reference checks are completed; a reference report is written by the search consultant and forwarded to the client; and, if the candidate requests a copy of the report, it can be made available. (Note: the search consultant is not required by law to make this report available to the candidate.)

Difficulty arises with the identification and disclosure of harmful information. If the search consultant is told "confidentially" that the candidate has been dishonest with financial reports or that he has a substance abuse problem, for example, does he confront the candidate? Share the information with the client as a "possible problem"? Simply eliminate the candidate and work only with the candidates whose references have raised no issues?

One industry practice is to consider only multiple reports that have repeatedly noted identical problem behavior. If a number of references identify a problem, confront the candidate. The problem may have been accurately identified, but it may be a past problem that has been corrected. Certainly the candidate has a right to clarify this issue. Does the client have the same right to be made aware of this past problem? With the consent of the candidate, I think so. The candidate cannot ask the consultant to avoid disclosing this information to the client, and the consultant would be short-sighted to do so.

If, however, the search consultant has not performed due diligence and reports inaccurate information to the client that causes the client to eliminate the candidate from further consideration, the candidate can (and maybe should) hold the search consultant responsible.

*Conclusion*

Referencing, like search itself, is a complex process. Success for both is dependent upon the good judgment of all the individuals involved, but it is orchestrated by the individual executive search consultant who is responsible for managing the process.

Many search professionals have developed a reputation for integrity and the highest of ethical standards. Find them. Use them.

JANIS M. ZIVIC, *founder of the Zivic Group, Inc., in San Francisco, has been a professional recruiter for twenty-three years. She was the first female president of the California Executive Recruiters Association and has recently been appointed Library Commissioner for the City and County of San Francisco. She also serves on several nonprofit boards in San Francisco.*

*Most donors and prospects cherish their privacy, yet some fundraisers believe they need to know "everything" before approaching a prospect. What are the ethics of fundraising research?*

# 7

# Ethics in the research office

*Beverly Goodwin*

FOR MOST OF US, trying to define ethics and then decide on guidelines for ethical behavior is like trying to herd cats. It is overwhelming. Definitions and interpretations dart all over the place.

How do we define and choose ethical behavior? In *The Hard Problems of Management: Gaining the Ethics Edge*, Mark Pastin (1986, p. 33) writes that the study of ethics presents "few black and white solutions; instead it offers complex problems, hard choices and uncertain outcomes." Development professionals must deal with these complex problems and uncertain outcomes almost daily. Consider this typical case:

The director of a university's capital campaign asks the research staff to provide him with a list of donors (and dollars donated) to the campus AIDS research project. Copies of the list are to be given to volunteer gift solicitors, most of whom are friends of those they are about to solicit. The volunteers will be asking for gifts for the hospital building fund. How should the research director respond to this request?

This is one example of the dilemmas a researcher in development work faces every day. Part of the problem is that almost no one but

NEW DIRECTIONS FOR PHILANTHROPIC FUNDRAISING, NO. 6, WINTER 1994 © JOSSEY-BASS PUBLISHERS

the researcher thinks anything is wrong with the request. How does the researcher in this predicament decide what to do? In this instance, the researcher faces donor-privacy issues, as well as the issue of dealing with the boss, who seems to have no qualms about distributing this kind of information.

What are the researcher's options?

Keep quiet, print the list for the campaign director, and make copies for the volunteers.

Provide one copy for the campaign director. He is paid to make decisions regarding sensitive issues like this.

Refuse to provide the list, making the point that donor records are confidential and should stay in-house.

Give one copy of the list to the campaign director, with a reminder about donor-privacy issues. Mention the organization's policy not to reveal donor records to anyone outside the office, including volunteer campaign solicitors. Suggest that policies be discussed and clarified at a staff meeting.

Why does this not seem to be a dilemma for the campaign director? If he is unaware of a problem here, some consciousness raising may be in order. If he knows it is wrong, why is he doing it?

Why would a person knowingly commit an unethical action?

Organizations tend to develop counter-norms: accepted organizational practices that are contrary to prevailing ethical practices (Sims, 1992; Jansen, Von Glinow, 1985). Such counter-norms, which may influence a person to commit unethical acts, include "accepted" practices such as the following:

• Organizations often reward behaviors that violate ethical standards. "I don't know what you had to do to get these gifts, but it's earned you a country club membership."

• Some managerial values undermine integrity. In a study on executive integrity, Wolfe found that "managers have developed some ways of thinking (of which they may be quite unaware) that foster unethical behavior" (Sims, 1992). "I want you to get me everything on this prospect." The person targeted would probably be upset to learn that the organization knows more than it needs to know about his private and financial affairs.

• Even though being open and honest is a preferred ethical norm, "within organizations it is often considered not only acceptable, but desirable, to be much more secretive and deceitful" (Sims, 1992, p. 507). "I know she wants to leave it all to the dog grooming school, but she's kind of losing it. How does the 'Fifi School of Engineering' sound?"

• Executives (and researchers) may be more concerned about their actions appearing ethical than by their actual morality. "Donors can ask to see their file at any time. Now, where is our shadow version of that profile?"

• Managers may not differentiate between what is lawful and what is ethical. "We use only legally accessible information for professional purposes. . . . Her driver's license says she weighs how much?"

• Behavior may be rationalized by pretending it is not really unethical or illegal (Sims, 1992, p. 509). "There's no need to dredge up all those old articles about our donor's hair-growing scam. Who can prove he used *that* money to fund the Hirsute Institute?"

• Behavior is excused by saying it is in the best interest of the organization (Sims, 1992, p. 509). "I think 'Mafia Gardens' is a fine name for our new botanical department."

• There may be too much pressure to reach a goal without an equal emphasis on following legitimate procedures (Cohen, 1993).

• There is an assumption that no one will find out.

• "Everybody does it!"

Some of these examples are tongue-in-cheek, but they do illustrate that there are many ways to slip into questionable behavior. How can we tell if our practices are leading us into areas that violate donors' rights? Robert Gellman, Chief Counsel for the House Committee on Government Information, Justice and Agriculture, speaking at the 1992 American Prospect Research Association (APRA) national conference, suggested this test: If telling a prospect how you obtained your information would make that person feel uncomfortable, or might cause a potential donor to withhold a contribution, then what you have done is probably an invasion of personal privacy. If you cannot be open and honest about the information you collect and the methods you use, then you may well be engaging in unfair information practices.

How do we choose an ethical path?

In our journey through the ethics jungle (or desert, depending upon one's view), how can we find our way? We can read the classics to develop a basic theoretical background in ethics, and we can collect materials to use as guidelines in making ethical decisions. We will find ourselves pondering the classic ethical issues in attempting to solve the problems of everyday life: Are there absolute ethical standards? How do the interests of our organization weigh against higher ethical standards? In making a decision, how shall we weigh the good against the harm we might do? How do we choose an ethical path when we are being pressured to do otherwise?

How can we learn about behaving ethically in the workplace?

Problem solving and ethics training can help employees to construct or clarify their own personal ethical framework. Training should be for all employees. Experienced facilitators might be brought in—not only for their expertise, but to create a receptive, nonjudgmental atmosphere for exploring ethical issues.

Playing out scenarios of ethical dilemmas before a crisis arises may prevent the occurrence of the actual dilemma in the future. Participation in these exercises may actually be more important than the resulting written code of ethics.

Forming an ethics committee (with members representing all areas of the organization) may be one of the most effective ways of addressing actual ethical dilemmas. Ideally, this would be a "safe" place where anyone could go with an ethical dilemma. Some of its functions would be to clarify, interpret, and test the established standards and policies of the organization. It would help ensure that decisions made are consistently based on these standards.

## Creating an ethical climate

Even though moral conduct is often determined by an individual's moral character, another critical determinant of ethical behavior is the work environment. The ethical climate of the work environment refers to "the pervasive moral atmosphere of the organization, characterized by shared perceptions of right and wrong, as well as common assumptions about how moral concerns should be addressed" (Cohen, 1993, p. 343).

The ethical climate is a product of the organization's culture. A number of studies indicate that the culture of an organization can influence employees to behave ethically or unethically. If ethical behavior is encouraged up to a point—until it begins costing too much—then it is known throughout the organization that a certain amount of unethical behavior will be tolerated, and employees will behave accordingly. When dilemmas arise in these organizations, unethical behavior will often result (Sims, 1992).

The organization should strive for an ethical work climate that is clear and positive, where all know what is expected of them when dilemmas occur. Many studies support the idea that the ethical climate is created by those at the top. The leaders must set standards, truly believe in them, and act on them. The way they conduct themselves on a daily basis sets the tone for everyone else in the organization. If they do not "walk the talk," others probably will not feel they have to either.

In "The Challenge of Ethical Behavior in Organizations," Sims

(1992) reports on research conducted over twenty-five years, which concludes that the ethical philosophies of management have a major impact on the ethical behavior of their employees. "How ethical behavior is perceived by individuals and reinforced by an organization determines the kind of ethical behavior exhibited by employees."

Others, such as Bill Roth (1993), maintain that there must be a holistic, systemic strategy that emphasizes a team approach. Roth asks, "Is it quality that improves ethics, or ethics improves quality?" He concludes that the dependency is usually stronger in the quality-ethics direction than in the ethics-quality direction. His view is that a team environment fosters ethical behavior. A quality-improvement team network encourages employees to prevent unethical behavior and has the authority to communicate its concerns through the network to all other stakeholders. Communication and access to information are critical to the generation and maintenance of high ethical standards. When the power for making decisions and accessing information is given to more people with their diverse perspectives, it becomes increasingly difficult for individuals to get involved in unethical activity. More people know what is going on, and the possibility of detection and whistle-blowing, a deterrent to unethical behavior, increases.

But Roth, like Sims, maintains that if an organization wants employees to behave ethically, it must first communicate very clearly what is expected of them. These expectations are appearing with increasing frequency in the mission or "vision" statements of organizations.

When employees know the rules of the game and feel free to communicate, they can identify changes that will help the organization as a whole. This increased emphasis on team approaches and more open communication (aided by e-mail and computer networking) may be the model for the future.

What part can the research office play in creating an ethical work climate?

The research office, with its unique position in the organization (meaning it has not quite been decided where it should fit on the flow chart) has the opportunity to be in contact with almost all individuals throughout the organization. If an e-mail system is in general use, the research office might send out mini-case studies for discussion on a regular basis. This already occurs among researchers using the *prspct-l* listserv on the Internet to help each other solve ethical problems. Hundreds of researchers in the United States and Canada communicate daily, helping each other with ethical and other research-related issues.

Typical ethical dilemmas can also be presented at staff meetings to give participants practice in looking for options when presented with problems. Games in which teams must agree on one multiple-choice answer to an ethical problem can be instructional and fun (such as "Gray Matters," developed for internal use at Martin Marietta).

## The work space

The physical layout of the research office may also contribute to the ethical work climate. If researchers work together in a general open area (with dividers) where they can overhear each other and help one another solve problems as they arise, they may be less apt to attempt to resolve sticky situations on their own. Talking things over with others may help keep decisions in line with the higher ethical expectations of the organization.

## Ethics issues in prospect tracking

When the prospect tracking functions are housed in the research office, a broad view of most development activities is possible. Rather than looking on tracking as a way for administrators to strictly monitor the cultivation activities of development officers, researchers may be able to act more like air-traffic controllers, helping everyone know where the others are and where they are heading. Potential problems may be spotted and collisions (two development officers zeroing in on the same donor at the same time) prevented.

This function has more appeal than the role of the traffic cop. The research office should not be in the position of policing anyone on behalf of administrators. Rather than waiting for problems to develop, and then pointing fingers, we may be able to defuse situations. Ideally, we can help everyone keep in touch and encourage cooperation. Studies have suggested that secretiveness and excessive competition between development officers seem to foster opportunities for unethical behavior. A prospect tracking system can probably be used most effectively as a tool for development officers to monitor themselves, rather than as incriminating evidence to be held over their heads by an administrator. Maintaining a neutral, open shop, where everyone feels they can come for a status report on what is happening in the organization as a whole, creates a less threatening atmosphere for most development officers.

For organizations whose policies and computer systems allow it, information needed by development officers and administrators should be personally accessible by computer from the research office. This, of course, brings up the necessity for having information policies in place so everyone understands the responsibilities that go along with the increased freedom to access information. It is this access and sense of responsibility that will be valuable in keeping the lines of communication open when ethical dilemmas arise.

Finally, issues of donor privacy and rights need to be considered foremost in the maintenance of a tracking system. Records need to be kept in such a way that you or the donor would not be embarrassed if the donor saw them.

Although there is more sophistication about fundraising in recent years, some people are still surprised to learn that nonprofits and educational institutions engage in careful background research before they call on a prospective donor to ask for a large gift. In just the past few years people outside the development field have become aware that there is such a thing as "prospect research." What they have heard has made them uneasy. Articles in *Newsweek*, *The Wall Street Journal*, and other national publications have not done much to calm their fears. They have learned that, often without their knowledge or permission, details of their lives are being revealed to others. Not only that, their trusted nonprofits and educational institutions are hiring researchers who specialize in going after this kind of information.

A few researchers will admit to some embarrassing things done in the name of research—copying down license numbers to track down owners of luxury cars, misrepresenting themselves when asking for sensitive public records—in an overzealous attempt to do a thorough profile on a prospect. In the heat of a large capital campaign, and under pressure to produce, a researcher may be tempted to do whatever needs to be done to bring home the big names. How far should he go?

Businesses, banks, and credit bureaus have been accessing, buying, and selling information about all of us, without our permission, to an increasing extent in recent years. They do this to make it easier for them to sell us something (or not) at their discretion. Why can't we do the same, with whatever meager resources we have, to benefit our struggling nonprofits and prestigious educational institutions?

Reactions to what we do as prospect researchers were offered by panelists at an ethics session of the 1992 APRA national conference. Mary Culnan, professor of business at Georgetown University and director of the Privacy and Technology Project for the ACLU, said: "Quite frankly, I'm somewhat appalled at what goes on, and I'm concerned about privacy. . . . Some of these are *prospective* donors we are talking about, not always those who have already established a relationship with us." They should be concerned because we are "out there digging up details on them because they have got money." Most people today have become accustomed to the idea that they are giving up some of their privacy in exchange for convenience (personal information in exchange for a credit card), but

APRA speaker Robert Gellman observed that it is going to be difficult to explain to people how they are going to personally be advantaged by the collection and maintenance of information for *your* purposes. "At least the direct marketers can offer to sell me a fruitcake, and there's a chance that I might like fruitcake."

On the other hand, a panel of philanthropists at the 1993 annual conference seemed to accept the idea that nonprofits do background research on a prospective donor. They were concerned that it be done with sensitivity and confidentiality, however.

Among researchers, the range of ideas about what is right and wrong is truly remarkable—probably as diverse as for the population at large. Staunch defenders of certain investigative research practices defend their right to access anything that is accessible, while others examine these same practices with a troubled conscience. In the rough-and-tumble of our spirited discussions, we are helping each other work out our rules to live by.

## Public versus private information

Here is where potential problems arise: researchers collect information from public sources—information that was gathered for another purpose. The use of this information for other purposes violates the principles that underlie all privacy laws. The problem is that citizens have little choice in disclosing information for public records. We are compelled to give certain information for the record.

Much of the information we deal with is financial information, which, along with medical information, is particularly sensitive for most people. "This is not the kind of information most people readily share with others, especially those they don't know. My guess is that the prospect would say that this is none of your business, and you don't have a right to know this" (M. Culnan, 1992, APRA Conference). At least two areas are of concern here: use of public records for purposes for which they were not intended, and the sometimes hazy line between public and private records.

Most researchers pride themselves on the fact that they use only public records in their research. However, they may unintentionally be violating the trust of individuals to an even greater extent than those who blatantly seek and use any information they can get. When people buy property, or register their car, or apply for a driver's license, they assume that the information they provide in this process is for the use of the agency recording the official registration. They are usually not happy to learn that, in some cases, businesses, credit agencies, organizations, and individuals can tap into or purchase these data bases. This practice has resulted in betraying the public trust, and has led to increasing concern about the erosion of personal privacy.

This presents a dilemma for prospect researchers. If we access this information, we are doing something that is allowable by law, but troubling to those who value personal privacy. If the prospect could receive the names of those who have accessed his or her records, would that affect our research activities? In a movement toward protecting the privacy of consumers and donors, many companies have voluntarily established privacy codes of conduct. Several organizations in the nonprofit sector have banded together and produced a "Donor Bill of Rights" (see Conclusion, this volume). However, this bill and other codes do not address this particular privacy issue. We still do not seem to be getting to the hard questions.

Until recently, most people were unaware of the vast amount of information available on commercial data bases. A more serious problem today may be that people are aware, but feel powerless to gain control over their information in all these systems. It does not matter to the public whether you are an "information cowboy" in business or associated with a philanthropic organization; they still feel a loss of control over their own information.

One of the everlasting dilemmas for the researcher will be the freedom-of-information issues versus the rights of privacy for individuals. We need to balance our desire to gain access to all information that we have a right to access with our duty to protect the privacy of individuals who may not want certain information disclosed.

## Determining where to draw the line

Speaking at the 1992 APRA conference, Mary Culnan cited Mary Woodell in offering a few tests to help you determine whether there is a problem with what you are doing: If someone asks, "Where did you get this information?" or "How did you get my name?" they have a problem with your practices. Would you object if someone were doing the same thing to you? If someone called and asked, "Why did you pull my mortgage record," would you be able to give them a good explanation? Would you mind an article on the front page of the *Wall Street Journal* about your fundraising practices?

## Use of information from outside sources

Information of all kinds is for sale. We can buy almost anything we want to know; there are lists by the hundreds: names of people and their salaries, cars, yachts, race horses, neighbors, addresses of condos, homes, what they paid for them—even the number of bathrooms in these homes.

In his book, *Privacy for Sale*, Jeffrey Rothfeder (1992) told us how he, a novice in the information-seeking business, was able to uncover surprising information about Vice President Dan Quayle and the very private Dan Rather. Since then, the more responsible credit agencies have tightened up access to their records, but it is still alarmingly easy to access a great deal of information that most people consider private.

With all this information just waiting to be plucked and popped into the briefcases of information-hungry development officers, how do we decide what we should take and what we should leave? Just thinking of the possibilities can give quite a rush to someone who makes a living gleaning information to be used for the ultimate good of his organization or even the "public good."

What do we need to know before asking for a gift—and what do we not need to know?

In a time when it is possible to learn almost anything we want to know about someone, we need to decide how far we should go in gathering information. What do we really need to know before we ask someone for a gift? What is essential knowledge to have about a prospective donor, and what is not? A practice in some development offices is to ask researchers to dig up everything possible on a prospect before anyone makes a call.

Perhaps we should try thinking more in terms of how little we need to know in order to make a successful request for a gift. Why should we know everything? Wouldn't a more spontaneous, honest relationship progress and mature if the development officer and others associated with your organization get to know the prospective donor through personal contact? Invitations to special events, tours of projects in progress, visits to your institution—all these produce opportunities to get to know people better and give them the chance to tell us where they are interested in spending their money. These kinds of things can be reported back to the research office.

Because we have the ability to access what many would consider personal records, it is imperative that we develop a good sense of how to handle ourselves and the information available to us. There should be something, other than the expense of getting the information, that makes us think twice.

Deciding how to deal with information inside the development office is difficult enough. Bringing volunteers into the process presents additional special concerns, concerns worth solving since our volunteers often have influence that we do not have in approaching a prospective donor.

What does a volunteer solicitor need to know?

A volunteer solicitor should know only the general range in which the prospect may be able to give, even though the solicitor may be asking for a specific dollar amount. If the donor has questions about his own giving record, the solicitor should have him call the organization or development officer for details.

The solicitor should have some idea of the donor's possible areas of interest in your organization. He should know if the donor has had some past involvement with your organization or other organizations.

He needs to know about several other funding opportunities at the donor's potential giving level, in case the donor is not interested in the proposal just presented. The solicitor needs good, current information about your organization and should have some impressive statistics at hand. He should know who some of the donor's friends and colleagues are, and who the donor respects and admires.

The solicitor needs to know that enthusiasm and commitment are catching (most major donors give for the joy of it). He needs to let the donor know that he can make a difference.

What does the volunteer solicitor not need to know?

A volunteer does not need to know everything about prospects before he calls on them. A volunteer does not need to know the details of the donor's giving history, which is the donor's business. A copy of the donor's gift record should never be given to a volunteer solicitor. Pertinent information should be conveyed orally, rather than in writing.

If we should use less, rather than more, information, what will be the role of the research office?

There are a number of ways the research office can promote the development effort:

Find good matches among prospects, volunteers, and key people in your organization (professors, doctors, project leaders, etc.) and development staff.

Ensure donor/prospect records are kept accurately, securely, and confidentially.

Maintain prospect tracking and cultivation records for use by development officers and administrators.

Analyze donor gift records, correspondence, and tracking histories for trends, trouble areas, and indications for future action.

Organize committees to identify prospective donors, establish procedures, and supply names for consideration.

Sit in on advisory board meetings and attend development functions to get to know donors better and to gain a better understanding of their interaction with your organization.

Gather information from a wide variety of public sources (newspapers, newsletters, arts programs, annual reports, corporate reports, directories) to form an idea of a prospective donor's interests and level of participation in other organizations.

## Confidentiality and trust in the research office

Even though we have little contact with clients, donors, and volunteers, we are concerned about the confidentiality of their information and their trust in us. Policies that promote that trust, such as the following, should probably be in writing.

Volunteers should not have direct contact with the research staff without the knowledge of the senior executive.

Donors, prospects, and clients should know that they can ask to see their own files at any time.

Donors should be assured that their records are handled with sensitivity and competence. The processing of records should be explained to them, if they wish an explanation. Internal policies should promote this trust.

Confidentiality in handling client and donor records must be emphasized. These records must not be accessible by anyone outside the organization.

Employees must be aware of the consequences of mishandling records or otherwise violating the trust of donors. If a staff member or administrator leaves the organization, the records are to stay with the organization.

Each member of the organization should be aware of his contribution to the development effort as a whole and take individual responsibility for making sure his part is done well.

## Ethical problems related to new technologies

New ethical problems have emerged with new information technologies. Computers are constantly increasing in power, speed, capacity, and ease of use. According to Gordon Moore, microprocessors become twice as powerful and half as costly every eighteen months. We are now struggling with understanding how to handle information under these circumstances.

Some of the issues we must consider if we hope to maintain control over the information entrusted to us are those of security and access:

How and by whom is access monitored?

Do our systems have levels of security requiring authorized access at each level?

Are passwords guarded and changed often by their owners?

Have the consequences of networking our computers been thought through?

What kinds of information can be faxed? (We do not always know who may be reading it at the other end.)

Who can request reports and lists from our records?

Are old printouts shredded before recycling? Are they held in a secure area before shredding?

What information can be uploaded and downloaded?

Who has the authority to enter and delete data? Who can print records? What information can students, temporary workers, and volunteers see?

Are computers in locations where they are not likely to be accessible by outsiders?

These are just a few of the problems to be addressed. Decisions made here will have far-reaching effects on the security and confidentiality of our records. These decisions should be given a great deal of thought at the highest levels. Unfortunately, issues like these are often left to the technical staff or even data-entry clerks. In other cases, the research office inherits these decisions. Even if administrators are not computer oriented, they must concern themselves with policies governing these areas.

Researchers know what they need in a system for handling information storage, maintenance, and retrieval. They are probably the most comprehensive users of the computer in the development office. The research office should definitely be included when policies are developed for the use of computer and communications systems. If the issues of privacy and access to information are well thought out in advance, some ethical dilemmas may be avoided in the future.

## *Where do we go from here?*

Let us not forget our goal. We are here not only to maximize the fundraising efforts of our institutions, but to help develop true bonds with our friends and donors. To do this requires that we trust one another. Whatever we do should promote that trust. Having reputations as high-tech super-sleuths may be nice, but it does not do much for cultivating mutual trust. Let us not be seduced by the easy accessibility of information. We honestly do not need to know or use everything that is possible to know about our donors today, even if the information is available.

As researchers or administrators, we need to keep the broad view, and not focus so minutely on detailed facts and figures about people. Let us focus instead on bringing our story to our prospective donors, for the purpose of bringing us together. When this happens, they can tell us about their hopes and dreams, and we can listen. They want know how they can make a difference. If we do our job right, we can help them.

## References

Cohen, D. V. "Creating and Maintaining Ethical Work Climates: Anomie in the Workplace and Implications for Managing Change." *Business Ethics Quarterly,* 1993, *3* (4).

Jansen, E., and Von Glinow, M. A. "Ethical Ambivalence and Organizational Reward Systems." *Academy of Management Review,* 1985, *10* (4), 814–822.

Pastin, M. *The Hard Problems of Management: Gaining the Ethics Edge.* San Francisco: Jossey-Bass, 1986.

Roth, B. "Is It Quality Improves Ethics or Ethics Improves Quality?" *Journal for Quality and Participation,* Sept. 1993, pp. 6–10.

Rothfeder, J. *Privacy for Sale: How Computerization Has Made Everyone's Private Life an Open Secret.* New York: Simon & Schuster, 1992.

Sims, R. R. "The Challenge of Ethical Behavior in Organizations." *Journal of Business Ethics,* 1992, *11,* 505–513.

BEVERLY GOODWIN *is director of research in the Development Office, University of Arizona, member of the board of directors of the American Prospect Research Association, and chair of the association's ethics committee.*

*Ethical fundraising management recognizes that the values of institutions and individuals can differ. The obligation is to reach a common ethical ground that clarifies what behavior is unacceptable and makes it possible to ask questions and seek solutions for difficult or challenging ethical issues in the development program.*

# 8

# Ethics and fundraising management

*Marianne G. Briscoe*

TO SAY THAT ethical management is successful management would seem so obvious as to require no proof or demonstration. Defense companies that charged government exorbitant prices for toilet seats and hammers or hid massive cost overruns in billings, universities that charged inappropriate items to their indirect cost ledgers, and federated giving programs that allowed leadership to spend excessively and frivolously have all paid heavy prices for their misdeeds. Some have been fined heavily or have seen leaders serve jail terms; some have been required by the courts to establish departments of corporate ethics, or found that public distrust makes it difficult to continue their core businesses. If excessive and frivolous spending leads to such results, why do organizations continue to cut corners and act illegally or unethically? What causes these transgressions in nonprofit management, particularly fundraising, and why do they seem so frequent? Why is there so much uncertainty about what constitutes ethical conduct in development?

NEW DIRECTIONS FOR PHILANTHROPIC FUNDRAISING, NO. 6, WINTER 1994 © JOSSEY-BASS PUBLISHERS

Most often nonprofit fundraisers act unethically because they want to get as large a gift as possible as soon as possible for their organizations. They are compelled, either by their supervisors and trustees or by their own drive to excel, to act in ways that harm themselves, their profession, their donors, or their organizations. There are, of course, instances of personal greed or intent to harm; but in the course of trying to raise money for a just cause, the judgment of even the best-intentioned fundraisers can become clouded in ways that lead them astray.

### *Blaming "management" for ethical failures*

At the Council for the Advancement and Support of Education's (CASE) 1993 Assembly, Kirk O. Hanson, senior lecturer at Stanford University Graduate School of Business, asked a series of questions probing why ethical errors in fundraising and advancement are made. Several hundred listeners selected one of six responses and voted anonymously on interactive keypads. In seconds these tabulations appeared in a graph on the projection screen (Hanson and Landes, 1993):

| | |
|---|---|
| Cutting corners to meet goals | 18% |
| Following orders | 5% |
| Covering up one's own failures | 17.3% |
| Poor decision making | 32.2% |
| System drives behavior | 18.9% |
| Changing public values | 3.4% |
| Misinterpretation of directives | 5.0% |
| No response | 0.3% |

Thirty-two percent of the voters were surely correct in viewing poor decisions as the root cause of most ethical errors; indeed, the other five suggested causes usually stem from someone's poor judgment. The real question is why people make poor decisions. This

poll strongly suggests that fundraisers believe the urge to cut corners, to cover up, and "the system" itself lead to errors. In other
words, these advancement professionals feel external pressures that
they say lead to poor decisions involving ethical errors.

These pressures are seen, of course, as coming from management. The importance of ethical leadership in institutional effectiveness is made plain in the criteria for the U.S. National Institute
of Standards and Technology's Malcolm Baldrige Awards, given
annually to those companies achieving the highest standards of
quality in products or services. Winners have included Motorola,
Ritz-Carlton Hotels, and a division of Cadillac Motors. Based on
W. Edwards Deming's total quality management theories, the
Baldrige Award jury has established a weighted scoring system for
a wide variety of management areas (Figure 8.1). Of a possible 1,000
points, 100 measure leadership, including values, management for
quality, and public responsibility. Another 300 points focus on customer satisfaction, including committing to, determining, and
achieving customer satisfaction results.

The Baldrige standards do not declare that companies must be
ethical to succeed, but the criteria clearly measure principles and
policies that embody ethical standards in profit-making businesses.
The message is clear. Effective companies do not necessarily have
vice-presidents for ethics, but they do infuse their management
with values-based standards for performance.

Baldrige Award-winning companies also place enormous emphasis on customer satisfaction. In fundraising, the customers are the
donors. Much of effective fundraising depends on keeping donors
happy, and one fundamental way to ensure donor contentment is to
seek and use contributed funds in accordance with the highest ethical standards.

The Baldrige program has two categories: one evaluates service
businesses; the other, manufacturers. Nonprofits are certainly service companies, but they differ from for-profit businesses in that
they exist not to earn money for investors, but rather to meet other
human needs: to heal, to educate, to provide musical performances

## Figure 8.1.  Scoring the 1991 Baldrige Award

1.0  Leadership (100 points)
   1.1  Senior Executive Leadership (40)
   1.2  Quality Values (15)
   1.3  Management for Quality (25)
   1.4  Public Responsibility (20)

2.0  Information and Analysis (70 points)

3.0  Strategic Quality Planning (60 points)

4.0  Human Resource Utilization (150 points)
   4.1  Human Resource Management (20)
   4.2  Employee Involvement (40)
   4.3  Quality Education and Training (40)
   4.4  Employee Recognition and Performance Measurement (25)
   4.5  Employee Well-Being and Morale (25)

5.0  Quality Assurance of Products and Services (140 points)

6.0  Quality Results (180 points)

7.0  Customer Satisfaction (300 points)
   7.1  Determining Customer Requirements and Expectations (30)
   7.2  Customer Relationship Management (50)
   7.3  Customer Service Standards (20)
   7.4  Commitment to Customers (15)
   7.5  Complaint Resolution for Quality Improvement (25)
   7.6  Determining Customer Satisfaction (20)
   7.7  Customer Satisfaction Results (70)
   7.8  Customer Satisfaction Comparison (70)

Total points (1,000)

of the highest quality, for example. The mission of nonprofits is itself value-based. At the end of the day a nonprofit executive will ask herself what progress has been made in eliminating hunger or suffering or in bringing great music to the community. Nonprofit executives, particularly fundraisers, live in value-driven worlds and are held to standards that exceed the expectations of a high-quality product or service produced and sold honestly.

## *"Stakeholder" analysis*

While fundraising managers encounter the same ethical dilemmas faced by most executives and professionals, they, like all specialists, encounter problems specific or endemic to their profession and field. Resolving ethical dilemmas in fundraising can be done using any of the several methods proposed by specialists in ethics: determining how justice can be done, determining whose rights have been violated, or deciding how the greatest good for the greatest number can be achieved (see, for example: Velasquez, 1982, 1992; Fischer and Associates, 1992). Each approach has its adherents and its uses.

The rights or stakeholder analysis approach seems the most consistently fruitful in fundraising situations. Fundraisers deal most often with four classes of interested parties or stakeholders: donors, their institution, themselves, and the general public. This last, which might be thought of as the abstract embodiment of philanthropy, is the most complex and should be considered the most important stakeholder. Philanthropy, derived from the root Greek words meaning "love of humankind," means altruistic behavior. In the fundraiser's world, this translates to contribution of time, talent, or treasure for the benefit of charitable institutions. Philanthropy, as managed by the fundraiser, exists within the public trust and within the tax code. American charitable institutions, under the code of the Internal Revenue Service, are tax exempt because they are viewed as existing for the public benefit. As Bruce Hopkins puts it, "they perform functions which, in the organizations' absence, government would have to perform; therefore, government is willing to forego the tax revenues it would otherwise receive in return for the public services rendered" (1990, pp. 2–3). Donors may deduct their contributions and charities need not pay taxes on their property or income (with certain exceptions). There is increasing public scrutiny of the roles of nonprofits, including fundraisers, in the "business" of philanthropy. A recent book, *Free Ride: The Tax-Exempt Economy* (Gaul and Borowski, 1993), was particularly critical of the large endowments and reserves, as well as generous compensation packages, found in the nonprofit sector. The legitimacy of the fundraising profession depends on the willingness of the public, particularly the philanthropic public, to allow fundraisers the privilege of "marketing" one or another cause or institution. People are perfectly capable of making gifts without the intervention or assistance of fundraisers. If the fundraisers are seen as untrustworthy or questionably motivated, the profession will lose its franchise. The first and primary stakeholder in an ethical dilemma in fundraising should therefore be the enterprise of philanthropy.

Donors, the agents or personal embodiments of philanthropy, should usually receive second priority. The importance of their claim must be weighted according to the degree of altruism in their motivations. Donors seeking no returns, recognition, or quid pro quo should have the strongest claim; those with more mundane motivations may be less creditworthy stakeholders. Generally, institutions take third priority, and the individual fundraiser should come last. One can quickly imagine situations where this ranking of stakeholders is unworkable or inappropriate; it is only useful as a general matrix for ethical analysis.

## Ethical decisions: Rarely black and white

When the fundraisers at the 1993 CASE Assembly conclude that most ethical errors stem from management errors, they show their basic human nature. Most of us will attempt to lay the blame for our own failings, ethical or otherwise, on the failures of others, particularly our bosses and leaders. It is, however, also fair and correct for fundraising managers to refuse to accept full blame and, further, to insist that every staff member has a duty to act ethically. All staff must work to prevent situations that result in poor ethical decisions. But ethical decision making is often difficult; it is rarely a case of divining clear right from clear wrong. What if a staff member must choose between refusing to follow procedures she or he believes to be unethical ("the system") and maintaining a good performance record (or ultimately staying employed)? What if the climate of leadership is such that bad news or disagreement with decisions characterizes the staff member as a "difficult" employee? What if a donor wants the charity to use funds for something not in the organization's best interests?

This is the first principle of ethical fundraising management: leaders must be prepared for questions, even challenges, of the ethics of their own decision making. They must practice discussing the ethical aspects of employees' decisions in ways that do not make either party feel insecure or threatened. They must create a climate in the workplace where values and stakeholder analysis are as much a part of decision making as fulfilling plans and meeting campaign goals.

There are risks to such openness. Ethical fundraising can be defined in many ways. Some areas are of relatively little dispute: the laws which must not be broken and the professional codes of ethics of such organizations as CASE, NSFRE, AHP, AAFRC, and APRA. Recently several of these organizations issued a "Donor Bill of Rights," which to some extent summarizes what ethical fundraisers and nonprofits must do for a donor (see Conclusion, this volume, for a compilation of these codes). The disadvantage of codes and laws is that they represent the areas of greatest consensus and therefore the lowest common denominators of our ethical thinking. They are good for the simple situations. None addresses the real frontier of ethics that one encounters in day-to-day decision making. What, for example, is the ethically right course—

When a planned gift donor refuses to consult her own, independent, legal, or financial advisers?

When an angry prospect objects to being interrupted by nonprofit solicitations during the dinner hour and calls the practice incorrigible (unethical) harassment?

When a trustee cries foul at requiring funds as well as volunteer time of its board members?

There is no good, universally applicable answer for the dilemma of the planned gift donor. But the angry prospect and the indignant board member are challenging widely accepted professional practices, perhaps from their own self-interest. So far, the dinner-hour phone solicitation is among the most effective donor acquisition and renewal methods and is protected by freedom-of-speech laws. The expectation that board members give time, talent, *and* wealth is a hallmark of effective nonprofits. Of course, telling the three people in the examples above that they are wrong will not resolve the impasse. Nor will capitulating to their strongly held positions.

In the case of the planned gift, the fundraising manager must first recognize that the situation presents a serious ethical hazard in risking the fact or appearance of undue influence over the prospect. The various professional codes of conduct are clear about this matter. So knowing, or making sure that staff know, which waters are treacherous can at least prompt the fundraiser to be highly circumspect in his or her actions. Circumspection does not mean acting covertly; on the contrary, it means acting in an unusually open manner so that those who could benefit from or be embarrassed by the decision to accept or refuse the gift are aware of the situation. Managers should refrain from "shooting the messenger" who has cultivated the donor and should participate in and support the necessary steps to resolve the dilemma. This means that the boss(es), not just the Planned Gift Officer, must take responsibility for any unpleasant consequences.

## *Values conflicts*

In the second and third cases, the fundraiser or manager is confronted with individuals who have value sets or standards of conduct that are not shared by the fundraising community. What is ethics to these people is, in fact, not at all an ethical issue to fundraisers. Such value conflicts are quite common. Some of our most vexed public policy debates circle the issue of taking human life whether through euthanasia, war, capital punishment, or abortion. Some people, for example, deplore abortion as murder; others agree that murder is wrong, but either do not define abortion as murder or see a higher value, perhaps the life of the mother, as taking precedence over the rights of the unborn child.

Whether or not to phone a prospect at dinnertime is of a decidedly lower order than the abortion debate, but one aspect of these problems is similar. One side focuses on the "rights" of the diner; the other says their rights are less important than another value, namely the right of the charity to present its case for funding at a time when this individual can be found at home. (Interestingly, we do not believe we should wake the prospect from his sleep, only interrupt his dinner.) The real issue is that the prospect objects to being asked on the phone and the charity persists nonetheless. This is a matter of tactics, not ethics. Fundraising managers need to understand the difference. Bad tactics can lead to troubles in fundraising, but they are not ethical dilemmas.

The manager who practices open communication about ethics must be prepared for what might be termed false ethical challenges not only from prospects and volunteers, but also from staff and senior management. There is much room for differing opinion about what is ethical once one is on the "frontiers" of the subject. That is one reason why ethics has been such a vital subject in academic and religious circles for millennia. Each individual, manager or not, must come to terms with his or her own ethical principles and be ready to work in a framework where not everyone shares his or her precise set of principles.

## Establishing an institutional ethic

This said, working to establish an institutional ethic is worthy of merit, and institutions do in fact have varied ethical standards. For example, it is generally seen as inappropriate for a substance abuse treatment center to approach its recovering clients for contributions, at least in a personally directed appeal. Yet hospitals, colleges, and museums routinely approach their clients for funds. There seems to be some level of confidentiality desired in treatment for drug addiction that is not seen in treatment for cancer.

Some organizations object strongly to fictionalizing "cases" in their fund appeals. "This SPCA doesn't need to make up stories about its good work," they say. "All cases should be entirely factual." On the other hand, health care agencies fictionalize cases as a matter of course to protect the privacy of the "real" clients whose stories they are telling.

Other organizations publish lists describing which clubs or levels their donors belong to, calling it a vital part of donor recognition that reinforces and enhances future giving and something the public has a right to know. Some organizations reveal the names of their donors only when required to do so.

Each of these instances presupposes a different level or kind of privacy to be accorded clients and donors, and different standards for communication with the public. Institutional policies and norms arise from the personality of the organization and its leaders, as well as the community in which the organization operates.

Bringing an organization to resolution about its own ethics can be stressful. It can require the best consensus-building skills of the fundraising manager and in many instances requires the participation of volunteer leaders whose value sets more closely resemble the interrupted diner and the angry trustee discussed earlier. A sharp and illustrative controversy in establishing an institutional ethic occurred in 1990 as the Sierra Club was planning a capital campaign to celebrate its 100th anniversary. One source of funding was to be corporate donations. As the campaign plan evolved, it became clear that several club directors did not want to accept corporate grants with "strings," which included no sponsorship grants for special projects. These directors wanted to limit corporate giving to unrestricted contributions. When it was explained that few corporations made unrestricted gifts of significant size and this would mean a greatly reduced campaign goal, the Sierra Club set about determining the terms under which it would accept restricted-purpose corporate gifts and grants.

The discussion quickly focused on which companies were "clean" enough for the club. The first review concluded that independent outdoor sporting equipment retailers seemed, as a class, to meet the club's rigorous standards. It was pointed out that such companies were generally so small they did not have the capacity to make gifts of sufficient size to meet the proposed corporate goal. In the end, the Sierra Club set a lower corporate campaign goal and established a Gift Acceptance Committee comprising "three wise persons," who were delegated the responsibilities of establishing guidelines to select corporate prospects, reviewing and approving every proposed prospect, and accepting or declining each corporate contribution received by the club.

For the Sierra Club and its community, corporations were a major source of the environmental degradation the organization is dedicated to preventing and correcting. As an advocacy organization, the club frequently lobbies against or sues corporations and their own lobbies. In the view of many club leaders, accepting funds from a former, current, or prospective adversary compromised the club's integrity and credibility, which were vital to its mission and goals. In contrast, corporate fundraising has gone on with no such concerns at United Way organizations, colleges, and research universities for decades.

Different ethical standards can and do coexist. It is the responsibility of the fundraising manager to draw relevant standards from the organization's subconscious and to have them articulated for the guidance and assurance of board, officers, and staff.

## *"Betting your job" on the ethics issue*

The Sierra Club discovered this was a stressful experience. In other cases, hammering out, or simply divining an organization's ethic, can be difficult or costly for the fundraiser personally. What does the fundraiser do when a CEO promises to build a building or carry out a program with a gift but has no intention of doing so? Or when a CEO sees no conflict of interest in instructing corporate counsel to put in order, at the organization's expense, the assets of a donor who has written a testamentary trust leaving the bulk of his estate to the organization? What about when a university is firm about its policy of investing in companies doing business in South Africa (in 1986), and the fundraiser believes in the Sullivan Principles advocating divestment?

He can quit in protest. She can attempt to discuss the issue with the boss. He can decide which ethical issues require taking a stand and pursue the first two alternatives only in carefully chosen instances. These may be cases in which the institution is clearly harming itself or others or where the fundraiser finds the issue so important that the consequences of whistle-blowing no longer matter. Ethical fundraisers must lead effective and productive lives in a less than perfect world. Not all challenges to personal standards should require a "bet your job" response. Both institutions and individual fundraisers must build ethical standards, but their standards will rarely be identical. Successful matches between individuals and organizations require that they are, at least, compatible and mutually committed to dialogue about ethical issues.

## *"Managing up" when there are values conflicts*

Fundraisers who choose to remain in institutions where their ethical principles and the ethical sensibilities of senior management differ must not abandon their principles. They have a responsibility to educate their CEOs, trustees, and fellow executives. This education is best undertaken with respect for the views of all parties and at a time and occasion distant from any event that triggered ethical conflict. "Managing up"—or educating peers, trustees, and bosses—needs to proceed with a recognition that few nonprofit leaders are intentionally unethical. They may have underdeveloped ethical sensibilities; they most probably do not understand or have not thought through the ethical concerns that apply to fundraising. Furthermore, fundraisers must be sensitive to the different ethical concerns of various management specialties. For example, the ethical standards followed by chief financial officers, college registrars, and even trustees have different emphases than do those of fundraisers. In Chapter Six of this volume, Janis M. Zivic illustrates the conflicting value sets between executive recruiters, the nonprofit community, and for-profit business. Here are two cases.

• A CFO proposed that the expenses of pursuing a major grant for a building be charged against the expectation of the grant and the cost of the building. The fundraiser objected: the prospective donor, a foundation, had clear guidelines that required their grant cover all building costs; fundraising costs were unlikely to be accepted as true building costs and could, as a result of the CFO's proposal, go unfunded anywhere in the organization's budget. Furthermore, the grant-seeking process with this foundation typically took as much as five years and there was small assurance that the charity would win the grant competition. The accounting procedure seemed quite reasonable to the CFO. After all, preliminary drawings, which might not be used in the actual design of the building, are legitimate building costs. So are financing costs. Why shouldn't the costs of seeking a grant be included in the building budget presented to the foundation? In short, they can't be because the foundation won't allow it.

• When an organization was struggling to close a six-year capital campaign with six months remaining and $6 million yet to raise, one trustee suggested counting some of the operating revenues toward the goal. Why not? It's all new money that meets the organization's capital and operating needs. Because the campaign promised to raise the money from gifts and grants.

Neither individual was acting venally nor did either realize his or her proposal was unethical. In the case of trustees it is an unprofitable strategy to reject their ideas as unethical in meetings with their peers. There are other, subtler ways of forestalling the unethical act and building more sophisticated sensibilities. However it is accomplished, the fundraising manager is responsible for educating such colleagues. Otherwise problems will arise repeatedly and the manager will fight continual rear-guard actions.

Effective ethics education will require more than diplomacy. Sound arguments for the positions fundraisers promote are badly needed. The importance of this point is seen in the National Society of Fund Raising Executive's (NSFRE) decades-long struggle to make its prohibition against percentage-based compensation an ethical norm in the nonprofit community. The Society's arguments on this issue are simply not understood, or are found uncompelling, by a large number of nonprofit trustees, directors, and CEOs. As a result, though members of NSFRE must refuse percentage-based compensation, the practice is widespread in the industry.

### Exercising the ethics muscle

Why is there so much uncertainty about what constitutes ethical conduct in fundraising? Perhaps it arises from our continuing search for rules to follow. There are some useful codes and rules, but they are inadequate for the dilemmas fundraisers confront in their variable and unpredictable environment. We will do better by looking for guidelines for recognizing areas of ethical risk (where codes can be quite helpful) and methods for resolving, as far as possible, ethical dilemmas. It is also important to learn that ambiguity, though perhaps not uncertainty, is a necessary condition for ethical fundraising management. In the face of such ambiguity, managers must develop the "ethics muscle" in themselves and their staffs, peers, supervisors, directors, and even donors. They must foster cultures where open discussion about ethics is accepted and encouraged, where there is no embarrassment for not knowing what is right and no blame for contemplating an ethically questionable course. There should, however, be a firm expectation that business will be conducted under the highest ethical standards possible. Employees who take actions judged unethical should be corrected or disciplined in a quiet, professional way. Peers and superiors who act unethically should become subjects for the manager's personal "ethics education program."

The ethical manager will also recognize that one reason ethical transgressions seem so widespread is that there are many, sometimes conflicting, value sets in which fundraising is practiced. An individual's ethics evolve and mature over time; there are certainly some constants, but issues that seemed of paramount importance in our youth lose ground to other principles as we grow older. There is similar variance among institutions and even among eras. Journalists are quick to defend what some consider their prurient interests in the sexual peccadillos of presidents and candidates. They say they reflect the new ethical sensibilities of our times—and the public is enthralled by their "investigations." Ethics works in the realm of the uncertain and the relative; it is an ongoing enterprise. While the ranks of fundraisers indeed include wrongdoers who should be stopped, a great many missteps occur through ignorance. Many more seem to be the result of collisions between value sets of individuals not familiar or comfortable with fundraising principles and the good and often thoughtful practice of dedicated development professionals. These are honest disagreements that, if they impact the practice of philanthropy, need to be addressed seriously and constructively. Effective management is ethical management; most fundraisers know and are committed to this principle. What we need is the discipline to exercise ethical judgment, that "ethics muscle," continually, not just as a separate topic at conferences, staff retreats, or other special occasions. Like all exercise, it is hard work;

but such exercise will bring substantial improvement to the health of the fundraising profession and philanthropy in general.

## References

Fischer, M., and Associates. "Ethical Decision-Making in Fund-Raising." Unpublished manuscript, 1992.

Gaul, G. M., and Borowski, N. A. *Free Ride: The Tax-Exempt Economy.* Kansas City, Mo.: Andrews and McMeel, 1993.

Hanson, K. O., and Landes, J. CASE 1993 National Assembly. July 13, 1993.

Hopkins, B. R. *The Law of Fund-Raising.* New York: Wiley, 1990.

Velasquez, M. G. *Business Ethics: Concepts and Cases.* Englewood Cliffs, N.J.: Prentice Hall, 1982, 1992.

MARIANNE G. BRISCOE *is a principal in Hayes Briscoe Associates, and former chair of the National Society of Fund Raising Executives Ethics Committee.*

# Conclusion

TO BE PROFESSIONALS, fundraising executives have to consider the ethical dimensions of their work. The authors of this volume have proposed substantial conceptual and practical issues that help foster ethical reflection.

While the context of decision making undoubtedly influences how we think ethically, several organizations are providing important benchmarks to assist volunteer leaders, donors, and professional staff in ethical considerations. The National Society of Fund Raising Executives (NSFRE), the most comprehensive professional organization for fundraising professionals, requires that its members adhere to the "Code of Ethical Principles and Standards of Professional Practice." The "Code and Standards" are provided here as a resource for readers and their organizations.

A second document that offers a basis of reflection for nonprofit leaders is the "Donor Bill of Rights," which was accepted by all the major professional organizations. The sponsoring organizations encourage all nonprofits to incorporate its principles in their own standards of performance.

Finally, we have listed eight organizations that offer additional resources that readers will find valuable. We encourage you to contact these organizations to further explore ethics in fundraising.

## National Society of Fund Raising Executives' Code of Ethical Principles and Standards of Professional Practice

### Statement of Ethical Principles (adopted November 1991)

The National Society of Fund Raising Executives exists to foster the development and growth of fundraising professionals and the

The National Society of Fund Raising Executives' "Code of Principles and Standards of Professional Practice" are reprinted here with the permission of the society.

NEW DIRECTIONS FOR PHILANTHROPIC FUNDRAISING, NO. 6, WINTER 1994 © JOSSEY-BASS PUBLISHERS

profession, to preserve and enhance philanthropy and volunteerism, and to promote high ethical standards in the fundraising profession.

To these ends, the code declares the ethical values and standards of professional practice that NSFRE members embrace and which they strive to uphold in their responsibilities for generating philanthropic support.

Members of the National Society of Fund Raising Executives are motivated by a desire to improve the quality of life through the causes they serve. They seek to inspire others through their own sense of dedication and high purpose. They are committed to the improvement of their professional knowledge and skills in order that their performance will better serve others. They recognize their stewardship responsibility to ensure that needed resources are vigorously and ethically sought and that the intent of the donor is honestly fulfilled. Such individuals practice their profession with integrity, honesty, truthfulness, and adherence to the absolute obligation to safeguard the public trust. Furthermore, NSFRE members

Serve the ideal of philanthropy, are committed to the preservation and enhancement of volunteerism, and hold stewardship of these concepts as the overriding principle of professional life

Put charitable mission above personal gain, accepting compensation by salary or set fee only

Foster cultural diversity and pluralistic values and treat all people with dignity and respect

Affirm, through personal giving, a commitment to philanthropy and its role in society

Adhere to the spirit as well as the letter of all applicable laws and regulations

Bring credit to the fundraising profession by their public demeanor

Recognize their individual boundaries of competence and are forthcoming about their professional qualifications and credentials

Value the privacy, freedom of choice, and interests of all those affected by their actions

Disclose all relationships that might constitute, or appear to constitute, conflicts of interest

Actively encourage all their colleagues to embrace and practice these ethical principles

Adhere to the following standards of professional practice in their responsibilities for generating philanthropic support.

## Standards of Professional Practice (adopted and incorporated into the NSFRE Code of Ethical Principles November 1992)

1. Members shall act according to the highest standards and visions of their institution, profession, and conscience.
2. Members shall avoid even the appearance of any criminal offense or professional misconduct.
3. Members shall be responsible for advocating, within their own organizations, adherence to all applicable laws and regulations.
4. Members shall work for a salary or fee, not percentage-based compensation or a commission.
5. Members may accept performance-based compensation such as bonuses, provided that such bonuses are in accord with prevailing practices within the members' own organizations and are not based on a percentage of philanthropic funds raised.
6. Members shall neither seek nor accept finder's fees and shall, to the best of their ability, discourage their organizations from paying such fees.
7. Members shall effectively disclose all conflicts of interest; such disclosure does not preclude or imply ethical impropriety.
8. Members shall accurately state their professional experience, qualifications, and expertise.
9. Members shall adhere to the principle that all donor and prospect information created by, or on behalf of, an institution

is the property of that institution and shall not be transferred or utilized except on behalf of that institution.

10. Members shall, on a scheduled basis, give donors the opportunity to have their names removed from lists that are sold to, rented to, or exchanged with other organizations.

11. Members shall not disclose privileged information to unauthorized parties.

12. Members shall keep constituent information confidential.

13. Members shall take care to ensure that all solicitation materials are accurate and correctly reflect the organization's mission and use of solicited funds.

14. Members shall, to the best of their ability, ensure that contributions are used in accordance with donors' intentions.

15. Members shall, to the best of their ability, ensure proper stewardship of charitable contributions, including timely reporting on the use and management of funds and explicit consent by the donor before altering the conditions of a gift.

16. Members shall, to the best of their ability, ensure that donors receive informed and ethical advice about the value and tax implications of potential gifts.

17. Members' actions shall reflect concern for the interests and well-being of individuals affected by those actions. Members shall not exploit any relationship with a donor, prospect, volunteer, or employee to the benefit of the member or the member's organization.

18. In stating fundraising results, members shall use accurate and consistent accounting methods that conform to the appropriate guidelines adopted by the American Institute of Certified Public Accountants (AICPA) for the type of institution involved. (In countries outside of the United States, comparable authority should be utilized.)

19. All of the above notwithstanding, members shall comply with all applicable local, state, provincial, and federal civil and criminal law.

## A Donor Bill of Rights

**(Amended March, 1993; October, 1994)**

Philanthropy is based on voluntary action for the common good. It is a tradition of giving and sharing that is primary to the quality of life. To assure that philanthropy merits the respect and trust of the general public, and that donors and prospective donors can have full confidence in the not-for-profit organizations and causes they are asked to support, we declare that all donors have these rights:

I. To be informed of the organization's mission, of the way the organization intends to use donated resources, and of its capacity to use donations effectively for their intended purposes

II. To be informed of the identity of those serving on the organization's governing board and to expect the board to exercise prudent judgment in its stewardship responsibilities

III. To have access to the organization's most recent financial statements

IV. To be assured their gifts will be used for the purposes for which they were given

V. To receive appropriate acknowledgment and recognition

VI. To be assured that information about their donations is handled with respect and with confidentiality to the extent provided by law

VII. To expect that all relationships with individuals representing organizations of interest to the donor will be professional in nature

VIII. To be informed whether those seeking donations are volunteers, employees of the organization, or hired solicitors

IX. To have the opportunity for their names to be deleted from mailing lists that an organization may intend to share

X. To feel free to ask questions when making a donation and to receive prompt, truthful, and forthright answers.

## Professional and Advisory Organizations

American Association of Fund Raising Counsel and
The Trust for Philanthropy
25 West 43rd Street, Suite 820
New York, NY 10036
212-354-5799

Association for Healthcare Philanthropy
313 Park Avenue, Suite 400
Falls Church, VA 22046
703-532-6243

Council for Advancement and Support of Education
11 Dupont Circle, Suite 400
Washington, DC 20036-1207
202-328-5900

Independent Sector
1828 L Street, NW
Washington, DC 20036
202-223-8100

National Charities Information Bureaus
19 Union Square West, 6th Floor
New York, NY 10003
212-929-6300

National Committee on Planned Giving
310 N. Alabama, Suite 210
Indianapolis, IN 46204
317-269-6274

National Society of Fund Raising Executives
1101 King Street, Suite 700
Alexandria, VA 22314
703-684-0410

Philanthropic Advisory Service of the Council of
  Better Business Bureaus
4200 Wilson Boulevard, Suite 800
Arlington, VA 22203
703-276-0100

# Index

Accountability: of fundraising profession, 37–41; as fundraising value, 54
Accounting methods, 71, 124
Altruism: as donor motive, 22–24, 110; of fundraisers, 42–47; and philanthropic mission, 109; recipients of, 25
Altruism maxim, 6–7
American Association of Fund Raising Counsel and The Trust for Philanthropy, 126
American Prospect Research Association (APRA), 90, 95–96, 111
Andrews, K. R., 66, 72
Aramony, W., 65, 71
Aristotle, 4, 5, 6, 12
Aspiration: ethic of, 16–17; gift economy as metaphor for, 18, 21–22
Association for Healthcare Philanthropy, 126
Audit, for ethical behavior, 67

Bakker, J., 65
Barnard, C. I., 50, 59, 60
Bell, P. D., 65, 72
Bellah, R. N., 31–32, 47
Bentham, J., 4, 7–8, 13
Bhide, A., 64, 72
Bloland, H. G., 33, 34, 47
Boards of directors: as donors, 112; personal involvement of, in fundraising, 69; role of, in ethical decision making, 63–73; role of, in ethical fundraising, 65–72
Bornstein, P. M., 33, 34, 47
Borowski, N. A., 110, 120
Bremner, R., 17, 26
Briscoe, M. G., 1–2, 105, 120
Buchanan, P. M., 42, 43, 45, 47
Bush, B. H., 38, 47

Callahan, D., 29, 30, 32, 47
Carbone, R., 42–43, 47
Caring, for others, 52, 53
Carnegie, A., 5–6
Carnegie Corporation, 9
Categorical imperative, 6
"Challenge of Ethical Behavior in Organizations," 91–92
Citizenship, 52, 54. See also Public service
Climate, ethical, 91–93, 97, 111, 118–120
"Code of Ethical Principles and Standards of Professional Practice" (NSFRE), 16, 26, 80; text of, 121–124
Codes of ethics: institutional, 1, 16, 114–115; of National Society of Fund Raising Executives, 121–124; professional, 1, 16, 29, 54, 80, 97, 111, 118
Cohen, D. V., 89, 91, 104
Coherence, in decisions, 59
Commitment, 54
Commodity exchange, 18–21
Communication: and decision making, 59; with/about donors, 92, 93; with management, 113. See also Information sharing
Community: and gift exchange, 19–21, 22, 23–24; in definition of philanthropy, 17–18; and public good, 29; types of, 22; and utilitarianism, 7–8. See also Public good
Compensation: contingency, for executive search, 75; incentive versus fixed, for fundraisers, 55, 69–70, 80–81, 118, 123
Competition, among fundraisers, 93–94
*Confessions* (Augustine), 12

129

# Ordering Information

NEW DIRECTIONS FOR PHILANTHROPIC FUNDRAISING is published quarterly in Fall, Winter, Spring, and Summer and is available for purchase by subscription and individually.

SUBSCRIPTIONS for 1994–95 cost $59.00 for individuals (a savings of 35 percent over single-copy prices) and $79.00 for institutions, agencies, and libraries. Please do not send institutional checks for personal subscriptions. Standing orders are accepted. For subscription sales outside of the United States, contact any international subscription agency or Jossey-Bass directly.

SINGLE COPIES cost $19.95 plus shipping (see below) when payment accompanies order. California, New Jersey, New York, and Washington, D.C., residents please include appropriate sales tax. Canadian residents add GST and any local taxes. Billed orders will be charged shipping and handling. No billed shipments to post office boxes. Orders from outside the United States and Canada *must be prepaid* in U.S. dollars or charged to VISA, MasterCard, or American Express.

SHIPPING (SINGLE COPIES ONLY): one issue, add $3.50; two issues, add $4.50; three issues, add $5.50; four to five issues, add $6.50; six to seven issues, add $7.50; eight or more issues, add $8.50.

DISCOUNTS for quantity orders are available. Please write to the address below for information.

ALL ORDERS must include either the name of an individual or an official purchase order number. Please submit your order as follows:
  *Subscriptions:* specify series and year subscription is to begin
  *Single copies:* include individual title code (such as PF1)

MAIL ALL ORDERS TO: Jossey-Bass Publishers, 350 Sansome Street, San Francisco, California 94104-1342.

# Previous Issues Available